The Old Mermaids
Wisdom Cards

Also by Kim Antieau

Old Mermaids Books
The Blue Tail
Church of the Old Mermaids
The First Book of Old Mermaids Tales
The Fish Wife
Magic, Myth, and Merrymaking: 13 Days of Yuletide the Old Mermaids Way
An Old Mermaid Journal
The Old Mermaids Book of Days and Nights
The Old Mermaids Book of Days and Nights: A Year and a Day Journal
The Old Mermaids Mystery School
The Old Mermaids Oracle

Other Fiction
Broken Moon
Butch
Coyote Cowgirl
Deathmark
The Desert Siren
Entangled Realities (with Mario Milosevic)
Her Frozen Wild
The Gaia Websters
Haunted

Jewelweed Station
The Jigsaw Woman
Killing Beauty
Mercy, Unbound
The Monster's Daughter
Queendom: Feast of the Saints
The Rift
Ruby's Imagine
Swans in Winter
Trudging to Eden
Whackadoodle Times
Whackadoodle Times Two
Whackadoodle Times Three
Whackadoodle Times Galore

Other Nonfiction
Answering the Creative Call
Certified: Learning to Repair Myself and the World in the Emerald City
Counting on Wildflowers: An Entanglement
Kim and Mario Build a Labyrinth and So Can You (with Mario Milosevic)
MommaEarth Goddess Runes
The Salmon Mysteries: a Reimagining of the Eleusinian Mysteries
Under the Tucson Moon

The Old Mermaids Wisdom Cards

Kim Antieau

Green Snake
PUBLISHING

*Dedicated to Mario, my sweetheart,
who always understood the Old Mermaids
and me.*

The Old Mermaids Wisdom Cards: Compact Edition
by Kim Antieau

Copyright © 2021 by Kim Antieau.

Special thanks to Nancy Milosevic.

ISBN: 978-1-949644-67-8

Published by Green Snake Publishing
www.greensnakepublishing.com

Contents

Beginnings *11*
The Five Seasons *22*
The Cards *27*
Sister Sheila Na Giggles Mermaid *29*
    Spring 37
    Dry Summer 38
    Monsoon 39
    Fall 40
    Winter 41
Sister DeeDee Lightful Mermaid *45*
    Spring 46
    Dry Summer 47
    Monsoon 48
    Fall 49
    Winter 51
Sister Bea Wilder Mermaid *53*
    Spring 56
    Dry Summer 59
    Monsoon 65
    Fall 67
    Winter 72
Sister Lyra Musica Mermaid *74*
    Spring 75
    Dry Summer 78
    Monsoon 81
    Fall 83
    Winter 93

Sister Laughs A Lot Mermaid 95
    Spring 104
    Dry Summer 108
    Monsoon 108
    Fall 109
    Winter 111
Sister Ursula Divine Mermaid 113
    Spring 119
    Dry Summer 121
    Monsoon 124
    Fall 125
    Winter 126
Sister Bridget Mermaid 128
    Spring 129
    Dry Summer 131
    Monsoon 132
    Fall 133
    Winter 134
Sister Ruby Rosarita Mermaid 136
    Spring 137
    Dry Summer 142
    Monsoon 148
    Fall 154
    Winter 159
Sister Sophia Mermaid 165
    Spring 167
    Dry Summer 169
    Monsoon 176
    Fall 178
    Winter 179

Sister Magdelene Mermaid *183*
   Spring 188
   Dry Summer 193
   Monsoon 197
   Fall 200
   Winter 203
Grand Mother Yemaya Mermaid *204*
   Spring 218
   Dry Summer 221
   Monsoon 222
   Fall 224
   Winter 224
Mother Star Stupendous Mermaid *226*
   Spring 228
   Dry Summer 229
   Monsoon 230
   Fall 231
   Winter 232
Sister Faye Mermaid *234*
   Spring 238
   Dry Summer 240
   Monsoon 240
   Fall 241
   Winter 243
Readings and Spreads *251*
Index *259*
About the Author *267*

Beginnings

Imagine a world where all is not exactly as it seems. A world where you are connected with the flora and fauna, the wind, the clouds, the rain, even the ground beneath your feet. You are an integral part of this world. The Invisibles and Visibles accept you as you are. You are a part of the mythos and the logos of this place. Such a place exists. It is all around you. It is in you. It is you. It is called the Old Mermaids Sanctuary. You won't find dogma here. You may find yourself, your true self. The Old Mermaids Wisdom Cards are here to help you do just that.

Every winter for more than a decade, writer Mario Milosevic and I stayed at Endicott West, an artist retreat on a piece of land just outside of Tucson, Arizona, near the Rincon Mountains. Endicott West was a place where artists of all sorts could find a temporary home in the wild desert while working on their latest creations. Mario and I fell in love with the place immediately. During the second winter we stayed there, I wrote my novel *Church of the Old Mermaids*.

I started the novel while sitting in the Quail House, a writing studio a short distance from the Main House. Inside I was surrounded by art and books; outside the amazing Sonoran Desert hummed with life. I could hear the constant wheat-wheat of a curved-bill thrasher outside or look out the window and see a Harris's hawk circling above in the blue, blue Arizona sky, all while trying to figure out where to begin.

I wanted to write the female equivalent of T*he Old Man and the Sea.* What would an elderly woman do to prove that she was still valuable? Something practical, I decided. Like picking up trash and helping people. With that thought, *The Old Man and the Sea* disappeared from my consciousness, and Myla Alvarez started telling me her story. It began with 13 "old mermaids" stepping out of the wash with their own tales to tell. They were all goddesses and all women just trying to get from one day to the next. It has always felt as though the land—the desert—gave me the story of the Old Mermaids. It was my job to get their stories out into the world.

In the novel, Myla Alvarez lives on and cares for a piece of land very similar to the land at Endicott West. Myla stays in the Bunkhouse in the barn and watches over the Main House and other houses in the area while the owners are away. She wanders the desert looking for trash that she brings with her to the Church of the Old Mermaids, a table she sets up in front of the local bookstore.

When people come by and express an interest in one of the pieces—like an empty bottle—Myla tells them a story about the Old Mermaids which usually begins with something like, "I don't know for certain, but I believe this (whatever it is) was used by (one of the Old Mermaids)" and then the story unfolds from there. If the person likes the tale, they put money in the Church of the Old Mermaids cigar box. Unbeknownst to anyone hearing the stories, Myla uses the money to help migrants she finds in the desert.

A month after I began writing *Church of the Old Mermaids*, I finished it, having written nearly every word in the Quail House.

After the book was published, the people who found *Church of the Old Mermaids* loved it in a different way from how people enjoyed my other novels. Readers were enchanted by the Old Mermaids Sanctuary and wanted to spend more time with the Old Ems. They understood that calling them "old" was an indication of respect. And "mermaids" harkened back to the ancient fish goddesses who were some of the very first goddesses in myth and folklore. People wanted to read more about the Old Mermaids

The Old Mermaids are young and old, different sizes, different skin colors, different sensibilities. Their whole world disappeared when the Old Sea dried up, and they had to adjust to living in the New Desert. They had to learn not only to survive in their new bodies and new home but learn to thrive. And they did. Not by hiding from reality but by facing it, learning new skills, and being there for one another and their neighbors.

Where For Art Thou, Old Mermaids Wisdom Cards?

I was changed by writing the novel *Church of the Old Mermaids*. I go through life now asking "what would the Old Mermaids do?" and then trying to be a bit more like them, not to copy them but to be more authentically myself. If all 13 of them decided on one mantra if would be the Delphic motto: Know thyself.

That's where *The Old Mermaids Wisdom Cards* come in. For many years, I wanted to create a tarot deck of the Old Mermaids and the Old Mermaids Sanctuary. The more I thought about it and tried to fit them into the wonderful symbolic tarot world, the more I realized that the Old Ems didn't belong in that world. They have their own stories and their own mystical, mythic, and magical ways. While some of them aligned with some aspects of the more archetypical figures in tarot, they are each their own person—their own being—while engaging in activities in their own community.

I believe what people really need or want from the Old Mermaids is their wisdom. We want to know how they learned to thrive despite losing their world. We want to know how they cared for each other and the land. Thus: *The Old Mermaids Wisdom Cards.*

Nowadays many people have lost the ability to tell the difference between reality and the imaginal realms. One can love stories and understand metaphor, analogy, and entertainment while still believing in science. As much as we may love the Old Mermaids, they do not tell us what to do with our lives; their wisdom and advice provide answers the way a great painting provides answers; their wisdom and advice provide answers the way a stunning dream can guide us to the truth. The path is our own: We make the decision.

Some Wise Details About the Wisdom Cards

The Old Mermaids live on a Sanctuary in a place very much like the Sonoran Desert only it is in the imaginal realms. Like our desert, theirs has five seasons: spring, dry summer, monsoon, fall, and winter. The Old Mermaids try to live in harmony with those seasons. Each season has lessons of its own.

In the Wisdom Deck, each of the 13 Old Mermaids

has a card for each of the five seasons. On each card is a photograph taken by me on the Sanctuary or elsewhere in the Southwest.

In this book, the cards are listed by the Old Mermaid in the order of their suggestions as they appeared in *Church of the Old Mermaids*. You can look them up in the index here if you prefer to work alphabetically. At the beginning of each section is a little (or a lot) about each Old Mermaid. Each section begins with her particular suggestion. Below the suggestion is the mystery associated with her. The mysteries are self-explanatory, but you can also find out more about each mystery in my book *The Old Mermaids Mystery School*.

Following this information section about the particular Old Mermaid, you'll find the cards that go with each season for each Old Mermaid. There are statements of wisdom and meanings for each card, but use them only if they're helpful to you. Over time, you might want to put in your own words of wisdom and meanings for the cards.

At the end of this book, I have suggestions for spreads. But one of the best ways of using the cards is to pick one card a day at random after asking the question, "What wisdom do I need today?" Then at the end of the day, you can choose another card, if you like, while asking, "What perspective do I need for the day?"

Some cards have stories with them, some don't. Some have a long explanation; some have a short explanation. More words does not mean that card is more important than a card with fewer words.

I use various spellings for the word used to describe the Invisibles or the fey. I spell it "fairies" when I'm generally talking about what we think of as the little people from fairy tales. I use "faery" and "faeries" when I'm writing about those beings and forces beyond the veils. It's a reminder to all that "little" fairies were and are powerful mythic energies that best be treated with respect. I also mix up the spellings and I capitalize other words sometimes and don't other times, depending upon the phase of the Moon and how I was feeling when I was writing. In other words, don't take it too seriously one way or another.

What is the Wisdom of the Old Mermaids?

They lost their world and had to build a new one. Although they grieved what had been destroyed, they were all interested in the present: They needed to know how they could survive and then thrive. They had to step out of their comfort zones and face a new reality. They had to learn all they could about their environment. They had to do this while they cared for themselves, each other, and their neighbors (human and otherwise). They lived full and rich lives while being their authentic selves. Isn't that what we all want?

Home is Where the Sanctuary Is

Mario and I currently own the place that was once Endicott West, the place where I wrote *Church of the Old Mermaids* and that became the Old Mermaids Sanctuary to us. I am writing about the Old Mermaids and the Old Mermaids Sanctuary on the same land where I wrote the original novel about a woman who lived in a place much like this one while she told stories about Old Mermaids who lived on land much like this land. I believe that's five-fold meta.

Pick Me, Pick Me! Or How the Cards Were Chosen.

I initially went through thousands of photos I had taken in and around the Sanctuary and the American Southwest. I looked for photos that would be especially clear on a relatively small card.

I also had in mind the 13 Old Mermaids and their personalities, the five seasons in the desert, as well as what I wanted to say about the Sonoran Desert (here and in the world of the Old Mermaids). Eventually I got it down to several hundred photos, then a couple hundred. Finally the 65. And then as we printed them, and as I wrote the book, I switched out photographs and put in new ones in some cards.

Most of the Old Mermaids tales here are original to this book, but some of them come from *The Old Mermaids Mystery School, The First Book of Old Mermaids Tales, Magic, Myth, and Merrymaking: 13 Days of Yuletide the Old Mermaids Way,* and *Church of the Old Mermaids* because some tales need to be heard again and again.

What is the Mystic Trail?

I see all of the Old Mermaid stories as mythic, magical, mystical and completely connected with Nature. In this sense, someone who is willing to step onto the Mystic Trail is someone who is willing to be devoted to and in awe of Nature. It is someone who tries to understand the Mysteries while also being willing to let go of the need to understand them. It is someone who understands that they do not know everything, and they never will. It's not about giving away one's self in the service of another: It is about being full of one's self while being a part of and in flow with Nature.

For me, walking the Mystic Trail is about a lifetime of longing for and communing with that which is beloved: the planet, Nature, the biosphere—whatever other name you wish to call it. It is not religious. There is absolutely no dogma, and no one can be hurt on the

Mystic Trail. That is one of the most important things to remember about the Church of the Old Mermaids, too: *There is absolutely no dogma.* The Old Mermaids are dedicated to each other, their community, and truth.

I Don't Know for Certain, But . . .

Most storytellers have a kind of cue or enchantment that allows the reader/listener to step on the pathway to the imaginal realms. The enchantment or cue lets them know that pathway is clear, and now everyone can go forward. In *Church of the Old Mermaids,* Myla uses an enchantment that goes something like, "I don't know for certain, but I believe . . ." and I carry that forward here in the Old Mermaids Wisdom Cards for many of the stories.

Where to Purchase the Old Mermaids Wisdom Cards

We have created three different sizes of TOMWC: regular tarot size, mini rectangular, and round. They all have the same photos, but they are sometimes cropped a little differently from one another.

You can purchase any or all of the decks at Make Playing Cards here: www.makeplayingcards.com/sell/old-mermaids-wisdom-cards. You can choose to have the deck in our custom box or not and you can decide whether you want the booklet or not.

We've also created two larger-sized editions of this book: *The Old Mermaids Wisdom Cards: Color Edition,* which reproduces the cards in full color at actual size, and *The Old Mermaids Wisdom Cards: Black and White Edition*, which reproduces the cards in black and white at actual size.

Have fun, and be wise!
Love to you all,
Kim Antieau

The Five Seasons

It's All in the Seasoning, Of Course
As I mentioned, the Sonoran Desert has five seasons. On the Old Mermaids Sanctuary here and in the imaginal realms, each season has its own special magic.

Spring (late February to April)
Spring in the Sonoran desert is full of new life, just as it is in most places at springtime. The birds are singing their lungs out, looking for love in all the right places. The snakes, lizards, and tortoises are shaking off their winter semi-slumber, and they, too, leave their underground homes and begin looking for love.

The Sonoran Desert is incredibly biologically diverse. Flowers begin blooming in the spring. If the desert has had a good amount of rain during the monsoons the year before, one can see blossoms nearly everywhere in the desert in the spring. With this new life comes energy and the possibility of new beginnings.

Meanings: new beginnings, growth, creativity, new ways of looking at the world, fertility, energy, youthfulness, socializing, new friends, new or rekindled passions.

Dry Summer (May to June)

By May, it is dry and hot in the Sonoran Desert. The cacti are blooming, along with desert spoon and ironwood trees. Nectar-feeding bats fly in to dine on night-blooming blossoms. Gila monsters lay eggs and those laid a year ago hatch now. Some animals begin to move to higher elevations as it grows hotter and dryer.

In June as it gets hotter, cacti fruit reach their peak, and all kinds of critters dine on them. Many of the legume pods ripen. Quail babies hatch out, and the parents are soon teaching them how to fly by hopping up into palo verde and mesquite trees. During the hottest parts of the day, birds hang in the tree, mouths open, wings open, as they try to beat the heat. Cottontails dig out forms in the dirt in the shade and snuggle down as deep as they can to find cool dirt.

This is the time of the year in the Sonoran Desert to learn how to survive. The Old Mermaids and their neighbors often went up into the mountains for at least part of this time, where they moved less, ate less, and talked less—except when telling stories.

Meanings: survival, learning to thrive on less, concentrating on the essentials, adapting to the environment, learning to go with the flow, finding your abilities and power to survive.

Monsoon (July to early-September)

Monsoon (or monsoon summer) is what they used to call summer rains. Now it's the monsoon summer. If it rains, it feels like a miraculous time in the desert. Some animals mate and reproduce again. The desert blooms again. More cacti fruit ripens, and the animals gorge on them. It is humid and wet and blustery.

If the rains don't come, it's a scary time. The flora suffers, the fauna suffers, people suffer. It feels like the end of the world. With climate change, monsoon rains have been absent some summers almost completely. In 2020, for instance, we had the driest year in history and the second hottest year in history.

When it rains, it is paradise, but the winds and flooding can be incredibly destructive

Meanings: hope restored, overflowing, passion, taking in what is needed, drought, perfect time to step onto the Mystic Trail, time when the veils are thin.

Fall (Late September to November)

The temperatures begin to go down. If the rains came, flowers are still blooming and fruit is still ripening, and the animals are still gorging themselves. The snakes that were hiding during the summer heat often return for a while before the cold weather sets in. Eventually some trees drop their leaves while others flash their colors before falling. It is a time of joy and comfort and relaxation.

Meanings: harvest, bounty, preparation for the future, socializing, relaxation, ceremony.

Winter (December to February)

And finally winter. Winter in the Sonoran Desert is when everyone can let their hair down, so to speak, and relax. The snakes, lizards, and tortoises, in general, go home to curl up for the winter. Tree fruits will ripen. Some birds will begin establishing their territories with song and nest building—like our curved-bill thrasher whose January songs should be recorded for all to hear. Hummingbirds often breed now. Some flowers bloom, like the fairy duster who shows off its pale pink spikes just about now. For the humans, we no longer have to worry about the heat as much. We can go outside without fear of dying of exposure if we're out too long. We can go with our own rhythms rather than having to adapt to the rhythms of the desert if they are not naturally our own.

Meanings: rest, rejoicing, planning, gratitude, an easy time.

The Cards

Sister Sheila Na Giggles Mermaid

Suggestion: **Get the starfish outta your eyes, sister.**

Mystery: **Be here now.**

Sister Sheila Na Giggles Mermaid is all about being here now. She has been known to ask people, "What's with all this time traveling? You're in the past. You're in the future. That's ghost territory. Be here now!"

Sister Sheila Na Giggles Mermaid is named after the European goddess Sheela Na Gig whose likeness adorns many old churches. She is often depicted as a skeletal woman who is pulling open her vulva for the world to see. She is most likely a goddess of life and death and may be related to the great Celtic goddess Cailleach who is the dark mother, the crone or hag-goddess, goddess of the harvest.

The Old Em Sister Sheila Na Giggles Mermaid wants us to get the starfish out of our eyes and understand reality. **Whenever you get one of her cards, she is encouraging you to be in the present.**

When the Old Sea dried up, and the Old Mermaids were tossed ashore onto the New Desert, they shook off seaweed, shook off the last drops of the Old Sea, hid treasures here and there along the banks, and whispered sweet nothings into conch shells that now littered the arroyo and looked like otherworldly creatures waiting for the command to come alive again and share their wisdom, beauty, and treasures.

The Old Mermaids grieved, some of them wailed, and some of them curled up on the sandy bottom of the wash like pill bugs awaiting a new and safer world. But one by one and then together, they eventually left the edge of what had been and what was now. They met their neighbors. They communed with the elements, with the Elementals, with the coyotes, jackrabbits, saguaros, and palo verde trees. They listened to the whispers of . . . everything.

Eventually they dug their fingers into the earth, added water and straw, and built the Old Mermaids Sanctuary. Where all were welcome. The New Desert had become home.

All the Old Mermaids had their place on the Old Mermaids Sanctuary. Sister Ruby Rosarita Mermaid was especially good at cooking—which was something since they had never cooked anything in the Old

Sea, except perhaps ideas. Sisters Faye and Bridget Mermaids were particularly skilled at figuring out the right songs to sing, the correct words for the enchantments, and the ingredients needed for this or that malady at this time of the year and phase of the moon. Sister Magdelene Mermaid was good at love. Grand Mother Yemaya Mermaid understood the mysteries, all of the mysteries, better than almost anyone or anything.

Sister Sheila Na Giggles Mermaid's sea chanties were quite colorful, and she could fix almost anything while telling a good joke. Sister Sheila Na Giggles Mermaid was mostly known for her frankness. Her honesty could make a person cringe, but she liked to say, "Get the starfish outta your eyes!" Face reality and move on, she'd say. Things will turn out one way or another.

Sister Sheila Na Giggles Mermaid adjusted to life in the New Desert quicker than any of the other Old Mermaids. Naturally, the area folks respected her—and kept her at a distance. Most humans do not care to hear the truth about the world or themselves, at least not as a steady diet.

But then there was Mary Connell. She lived on the other side of the ridge, near where Granita Wash crosses Coyote Arroyo. Over time, the community had become concerned about Mary. The Healer and Sisters

Bridget and Faye Mermaids had all visited her several times to treat her injuries. Rocks kept falling down on the path she took from her house to everywhere else. They fell on the path, and they fell on her.

This path, this trail, had been there for as long as anyone could remember. Mary Connell said her parents had walked that path every day of their lives. So had her grandparents. It was part of her heritage. Every year—twice a year—her father and her grandmother before him had cleared the path of rocks that had fallen from above. Some people cleared leaves and roots from their acequia twice a year; the Connells cleared rocks off their path twice a year.

It was not an easy task, but it was a possible task. Until lately. Lately the rocks fell more often, and it became a never-ending task to keep the path clear. Sometimes the rocks fell while Mary Connell was clearing the path. She had been struck several times.

"Will you go speak with her?" Sister Faye Mermaid asked Sister Sheila Na Giggles Mermaid. "We have tried, but she won't listen to us."

Sister Sheila Na Giggles Mermaid couldn't imagine what she could say that everyone else hadn't said, but she walked to Mary Connell's place one beautiful blue sky spring day. A coyote followed her partway, and a roadrunner ran ahead of her.

She arrived at Mary's house mid-morning, but no

one was about, so she walked down the path toward the garden, the path that ran midway along a rocky hill. Above was a ridge; below was desert scrub. Sure enough, Mary Connell was bent over a pile of rocks on the path.

"Good morning," Sister Sheila Na Giggles Mermaid said.

Mary Connell stood upright and leaned on her shovel.

"Good morning to ya," Mary said. "I'd invite you for tea, but I need to get this finished up so I can get to the garden before it's too hot."

"I can go to the garden with you," Sister Sheila Na Giggles Mermaid said. She looked down the hill a bit and saw an animal trail. "Look, we can go that way, go around the rocks."

"How does that solve anything?" Mary asked. "The rocks will still be here."

"But Mary, they are falling daily now," Sister Sheila Na Giggles Mermaid said. "This is all you're doing these days, isn't it?"

"And what of it?" Mary asked. She leaned over, dug her shovel into the rock pile, and then lifted rocks into her wheel barrow. "You work hard, you get things done. You work harder, you get better at whatever you're doing."

"You are certainly working hard. Are you getting better at moving the rocks?"

Mary shook her head. "No. I don't understand it. My father did this. My grandmother did this. I spend a lot of my time removing these rocks, but they keep coming back. I must be doing something wrong."

"Have you thought about moving the path?" Sister Sheila Na Giggles Mermaid asked. "I see the animals are now walking down further. To get away from the falling rocks, maybe."

"Or maybe they're just lazy," Mary said.

"You think the animals could move these rocks if they wanted to?"

"Maybe." Mary was breathing hard and sweating like nobody's business.

Sister Sheila Na Giggles Mermaid laughed. "Mary Connell, I didn't know you had a sense of humor."

Mary stopped and looked at her. "I wasn't joking. Look, this is my job. This is my heritage. It's something I've wanted to be good at my whole life. If I can't get to the garden, if I can't get to the well, then my life is over, essentially. So I have to keep the path clear."

"Or move the path," Sister Sheila Na Giggles Mermaid said again. She felt like she was talking to a stone.

"My father walked this way," Mary said. "And my grandmother. It is my heritage."

Sister Sheila Na Giggles Mermaid shook her head. "Mary Connell, more rocks are falling. It isn't gonna change for a while. That lightning strike up top last spring burned down two of the trees that were holding a lot of those rocks in place."

"I know," Mary Connell said. "I wonder if I should go talk to the Old Woman and Old Man of the Mountains. Maybe they can make the rocks stay up where they belong."

"They cannot change gravity," Sister Sheila Na Giggles Mermaid said. "I will help you move the path. It won't take much since the animals have already started it. And the rocks stop here on the path or in that ditch. They're not going down to the animal path. See?"

Mary looked where Sister Sheila Na Giggles Mermaid pointed.

"I've been doing this for years," Mary said. "If I quit now, maybe I'm quitting just before I get to that point where I will figure out how to do it."

"You're not quitting," Sister Sheila Na Giggles Mermaid said. "You are changing the way you're doing it. You'd just be stepping off the old path a little. In fact, it would mean that you did figure out a better way to do it."

"If I do it differently, doesn't that mean I'm saying my father and grandmother did it wrong?"

Sister Sheila Na Giggles Mermaid tilted her head. She did not understand this. She said, "No, they did it correctly under their circumstances. You have new circumstances. So you can decide: Do you want to spend your life on this path, shoveling rocks that are in your way, or do you want to change the path you're on and avoid the rocks?"

"It'll mean I won't be working as hard," Mary said.

"That's a good thing," Sister Sheila Na Giggles Mermaid said.

"Is it?"

Sister Sheila Na Giggles Mermaid nodded. "In this case, it definitely is. And it might save your life. You don't want to get hit by any more rocks."

"Well, there's no guarantee I won't ever get hit by any rocks," Mary Connell said.

"That be true."

Mary Connell dropped her shovel on top of the rocks in the wheel barrow.

"All right," she said. "I'm ready to change this trail. But first, let's eat lunch. I'm so hungry. You'll join me?"

"I never turn down an invitation to lunch. Whatcha got?"

"Stone soup, of course," Mary Connell said.

Sister Sheila Na Giggles Mermaid laughed. "There's that humor again, Mary Connell."

Mary Connell shrugged as they walked away from the rocks, down the path toward her house. "Who says I'm joking?"

Spring
Sister Sheila Na Giggles Mermaid
Wisdom: **Be attentive now.**

Lizards are everywhere on the Old Mermaids Sanctuary for most months of the year. These desert spiny lizards (Sceloporus magister) are probably the most colorful. The males are more brightly colored than the females, and they both get darker when it's cooler out. (It's called metachromatism.)

When it's very hot, they go underground or find shade to cool down, and they hibernate in the cooler weather. They primarily eat insects. The males do pushups. Some scientists say it's a way to attract females; others speculate it's a way to intimidate. Since they have done this when I've come near them many times, I'm assuming they are trying to intimidate me, not date me. Like most lizards, the desert spiny lizard can lose its tail and regrow it—although the new tail is not as big or as colorful as the old one.

Lizards can be very still, especially in the summer, maybe to preserve their energy in the heat. During the spring, they run like something on fire. Yet when they are still they appear to be aware of everything around them.

Meanings: Spring is a time of growth and creativity. The lizard can be very still, or it can run around looking for shelter and safety. It can be bold and colorful or it can be less colorful, more invisible. No matter what: It is always attentive. Do you need to be still, do you need to do pushups to allure or intimidate, do you need some color? You get to decide. Be here now and pay attention to it all.

Dry Summer
Sister Sheila Na Giggles Mermaid
Wisdom: **Be at home now.**

Sister Sheila Na Giggles Mermaid doesn't try to avoid the discomfort of dry summer. In the card, a hat is on a hook. Next to it is a wind chime. Sometimes, during certain situations—like the dry hot summer—we just have to get through it. Take off your hat, sit a spell, and listen to the wind through the chimes until you're on the other side of summer.

Meanings: Whatever is happening, just get through it.

You can do it. Try to be present for it. Be at home. One way or another, whatever it is, it will not last forever.

Monsoon
Sister Sheila Na Giggles Mermaid
Wisdom: Be a mystic now.

The veils are thin during the monsoon rains. This is a perfect time for you to step onto the Mystic Trail. A mystic is an initiate into the mysteries, one who walks the path of mystery and contemplation. What is Nature telling you? Dawn and dusk are betwixt and between times. One world is slipping away and another is coming into being, every day. In this card, it is dusk, dusk with a double-rainbow stretching over an Old Mesquite. Magic is definitely afoot.

The Old Mermaids understood that dawn and dusk are mystical times. Beginnings and endings are part of the Wheel of Life.

Meanings: Perhaps you are being called to the mysteries. What are the mysteries of life and death? Or maybe you are being called to recognize those times when the veils are thin. The double rainbows are wishing you good luck and maybe bringing you good luck. What would your pot of gold be at the end of the rainbow?

Fall
Sister Sheila Na Giggles Mermaid
Wisdom: **Be part of the clean-up crew now.**

Turkey vultures are amazing birds who can smell carrion from a mile away. They have excellent immune systems and can feast on all kinds of carrion without picking up any diseases like botulism, anthrax, cholera, etc. They use body posture to communicate. People are often disgusted by carrion-eaters, yet these turkey vultures are called nature's clean-up crew for a reason: They carry out the important work of cleaning up the environment after death.

I don't know for certain, but I believe . . . the Old Mermaids and Old Neighbors celebrated the vultures every fall. This yearly feast was started by AnnaMarie, one of the Old Neighbors who loved vultures. She called it Vulture Appreciation Day. The Old Ems and Old Neighbors travelled to one of the nearby canyons, Vulture Canyon, with picnic baskets for the Old Mermaids and Old Neighbors and carrion for the vultures, usually found by AnnaMarie or her husband. Sister

Sheila Na Giggles Mermaid or AnnaMarie gave a short speech before they ate, lauding the vultures for doing their "dirty work."

"Thank you for not turning away from death," Sister Sheila Na Giggles Mermaid would say. "We appreciate you eating it for us."

Then they all ate and sang while the vultures watched from their perches on the rocks above before eventually coming down to eat.

Meanings: Fall is a time to socialize and appreciate all that is around us. Appreciate those people in our lives who clean-up. Become part of the clean-up crew: Pick up garbage or do those chores that no one else wants to do. If you are usually part of the "clean-up crew," give yourself applause and take a break. Vultures are important members of the community for the dirty work they do; emulate them.

Winter
Sister Sheila Na Giggles Mermaid
Wisdom: **Be a hunter now.**

Roadrunners are omnivores who are efficient hunters. When we see one around the Sanctuary, it almost always has a lizard hanging from its mouth. They live alone or in pairs and are apparently monogamous. During mating and nesting season, the male does a bit of a dance for the female, his tail going around and around. He calls out and may even have food for her. This year the male roadrunner did his dance with a lizard hanging out of his mouth. The female seemed to like it because she flew down from the tree, and then they mated—with the lizard still in the male roadrunner's mouth.

I can't know for sure, but I believe . . . the roadrunners often disappeared in the winter. No one was sure where they went. Then one day—maybe it was Solstice; maybe it wasn't—Sister Sheila Na Giggles Mermaid was walking in the wash, and she saw what looked like a shimmering silver curtain draped across the wash. It was there and then it was gone, there and then gone. She had seen it before. She knew magic was coming her way.

Sure enough, the nowhere curtains turned blue-green, and two very tall and very thin figures shot through them, tumbled into the wash, and landed almost right in front of her. They wore colorful shirts and short pants with dark blue-green feathers sticking out everywhere. Their beaks were long and ferocious-looking, their eyes red, the feathers around their face orange and red, blue, green, and purple. They were stunningly beautiful.

Sister Sheila Na Giggles Mermaid thought, "So

this is what happens to roadrunners in the winter! They become faeries."

"Hello, good Old Mermaid," one of them said.

"Have you come to hunt prey?" Sister Sheila Na Giggles Mermaid asked. She hoped the answer was no.

The roadrunners laughed.

"Goodness, no," the one with blue feathers over its eyes said. "But we are here to hunt, of course."

"Naturally," the other said.

"Naturally," Sister Sheila Na Giggles Mermaid said. "What are you hunting for?"

"A good time," the roadrunners said together.

Sister Sheila Na Giggles Mermaid laughed. "That we can show you. Come with me. We've got good stories to tell, and I bet you do too."

"First we want to race up that mountain," Blue Feathers said. "Would you like to join us?"

Sister Sheila Na Giggles Mermaid shook her head. "Not today. I'll watch from the Sanctuary."

All the Old Ems watched as the faery roadrunners ran up the mountain, their tail feathers glittering gold, purple, and blue in the twilight sun. After they ran down again, they sat in the back of the Old Mermaids Sanctuary house, around the pool, with the Old Mermaids and ate whatever food the Old Ems brought them.

"Thank you!" Blue Feathers said. "This is almost as good as rattlesnake."

"Don't be rude," said the Other. "It is as good as rattlesnake."

"Sure, sure," Blue Feathers said. "But if you want me to go find you a rattlesnake to cook—"

"No, no," the Old Ems said as one.

Blue Feathers shrugged. "All right. But let me tell you about the last time I battled a rattlesnake . . ."

Meanings: Winter is a relaxing time of the year in the Sonoran Desert. Relax into your imagination. See if you can hunt down a good time.

Sister DeeDee Lightful Mermaid

Suggestion: **Step lightly. Dance hard. Eat your vegetables.**

Mystery: **Be full of yourself.**

Sister DeeDee Lightful Mermaid is full of herself in the best possible way, in the way we should all be full of ourselves. If not full of ourselves, who else? She has a difficult time at first when the sisters wash ashore in the New Desert, but she figures it out. She sees the light, as it were. **No matter what Sister DeeDee Lightful Mermaid card you get, remember that at the heart of each one is the question: How best can I be true to myself?** The greatest gift we can give the world is our authentic selves.

Spring
Sister DeeDee Lightful Mermaid
Wisdom: Be yourself and transform.

Two blue swallowtail butterflies on a blooming barometer bush/Texas sage beautify this card. The Texas sage is a member of the figwort family and is not a true sage plant. We also call it a barometer bush because it often blossoms before a rain. It seems to know when it is going to rain before any of us do. For most of the year, these bushes are relatively dull-looking, with silver or pale green leaves, and then suddenly, they sniff out water or some change in the Universe, and flowers pop out all over them.

Sometimes when I look at this photo, it seems as if the top butterfly is coming out of the bottom one, as though the soul of the butterfly is now taking flight. Butterflies are such amazing creatures. Maybe their souls can be made visible. Think about it: They are worms that form a chrysalis around themselves and then they essentially turn to goo, and then, voila, they are butterflies. They are the epitome of transformation.

The Old Mermaids honored butterflies and barometer bushes. Both were able to transform themselves, even when under stress, which is exactly what the Old

Mermaids did when they left the Old Sea and ended up in the New Desert.

Meanings: Be yourself and transform. It's spring. Be full of light and life—and yourself. Bloom! Rain is coming to nourish you. Let yourself change.

Dry Summer
Sister DeeDee Lightful Mermaid
Wisdom: **Speak up for yourself.**

When it is hot and dry and over 100 degrees, birds sometimes come up to our windows, hang onto the ledges, and peer inside. They may do this all over the house, but we notice it on our office windows which are on the east side of the house. They don't seem afraid of us; they appear curious.

The birds that come to our windows are usually cactus wrens or these little brown jobs who are called lbjs when birdwatchers aren't really certain what kind of bird they are. I think this is a black-tailed gnatcatcher, but it might be a female verdin. Or something else completely.

Maybe the window is cooler than the rest of the world in the summer. Maybe there are bugs on the window it wants. Or perhaps when we think the bird is looking at us, it is just staring at its own reflection, thinking, "what a beauty." Sometimes I fear they are really hot and want water. We've put water all around the Sanctuary, so I'm hoping that's not it. But we don't know why they come to the window, and we probably will never know.

The Old Mermaids left out water for the birds, too, just like we do. They recognized that sometimes we need a little help, even if we are a wild thing.

Meanings: You might need help. If so, make certain you speak up. Articulate your needs because no one can read your mind, not even lbjs.

Monsoon
Sister DeeDee Lightful Mermaid

Wisdom: **Step onto the Mystic Trail your way.**

At last the rains have come. The air is humid again. Hope is restored. Look to the red rocks and blue sky for answers. This is a perfect time to consider stepping onto the Mystic Trail. Be full of yourself as you do so, and do it your own way.

Meanings: The veils are thin. Consider the sacred blue sky. Consider the sacred red land. What can you learn from them? Can they learn anything from you? Take some time for stillness. Even as you step onto the Mystic Trail.

Fall
Sister DeeDee Lightful Mermaid
Wisdom: Keep on open mind.

This is the datura flower. It belongs to the Solanaceae family or what we commonly call nightshade. It is native to our continent, but it spread to the Old World as plants are wont to do. Despite its toxicity, it has been utilized medicinally for centuries, specifically for respiratory problems in many instances. It has also been used culturally by some Native American tribes. It is called thorn apple, jimsonweed, and moon flower.

In his book *Pharmako Gnosis: Plant Teachers and the Poison Path*, poet, ethnobotanist, and novelist Dale Pendell writes extensively about the rich history of datura. He mentions it in relationship to the Inquisition, puberty rites, Kali-followers, Georgia O'Keefe, the Chumash people, and Carlos Castaneda. Pendell writes, "Datura may be the single most dangerous visionary plant in North America. Well, maybe after tobacco."

According to Pendell, the Chumash used datura root sometimes to seek a dream helper. "The dream helpers come from the First World, which existed before the First People became all the plants and animals that we know today. Since the dream helpers are supernatural, and from the other world, one usually has to get away from this world to find them." Thus they took a datura root decoction. "The Chumash use the female plant. You have to learn from them how to distinguish the genders."

I took this photo of a datura growing along a river in a canyon near the Sanctuary. It felt like some kind of grove, even though I understand that word is used when talking about trees. The entire area around these flowers felt full: As though so much more was going on than I could comprehend. As I snapped photos, I thanked the flowers again and again. While I most likely would not ingest datura, I will listen to her and drink in her beauty and wisdom.

The Old Mermaids understood the magic and power of everything, including plants. Some plants were to look at, some to eat, some to learn from. Sister DeeDee Lightful Mermaid met Mother Datura on one of her full moon walks. Mother Datura was made of darkness, but the dress she wore shined, and Sister DeeDee was certain it was made of stars. She wished Mother Star Stupendous Mermaid was there to see it.

"Are you the moon," Sister DeeDee Lightful Mermaid asked, "come to visit?"

"Perhaps the dark side of it," Mother Datura said. And when she spoke a blossom fell from her mouth and planted itself in the ground and instantly became a glowing white trumpet-like flower. Naturally, Sister DeeDee Lightful Mermaid was delighted to see this. She clapped and asked for more.

Mother Datura told Sister DeeDee Lightful Mermaid many things, but it was wisdom only for her ears. The other Old Mermaids came and spoke with Mother Datura at other times. Almost everything they learned was for each of them only. They did each share that she said the best thing they could ever learn was "you don't know everything."

Meanings: Be full of yourself and understand you don't know everything. Do you need some wisdom of an elder, a flower elder? You don't need to take a hallucinogen to commune with great flower beings. You can also just talk with them and listen to what they have to say. Maybe ask for a dream helper.

Winter
Sister DeeDee Lightful Mermaid
Wisdom: **Give yourself a break.**

This is a time to sit back and relax. Maybe invite a friend to sit with you. You can look skyward and wonder what it's all about or you can watch the cottontails playing nearby. Once you rest and relax, you can fill up on yourself. Be full of yourself.

Meanings: Try not to stress. Sometimes being ourselves is not the easiest road. Our friends and family often want us to be like them not ourselves. Ignore that pressure. Give yourself a break, literally. Enjoy your own delightfulness.

Sister Bea Wilder Mermaid

Suggestion: **Things change. Get over it.**

Mystery: **Embrace the wild.**

Sister Bea Wilder Mermaid's name says it all. Her way of being in the world is all about being in the wild, in nature, and a part of nature. Her personality also encompasses the word "bewilder." To bewilder originally meant to lead astray, i.e. to lead one into the wilderness, as it were, away from polite society and stifling routines. **Whatever Sister Bea Wilder Mermaid card you get in whichever season, she is inviting you to come along for a wild ride.** It's not chaotic: It is wild and natural.

When she and the Old Mermaids land in the New Desert, Sister Bea Wilder Mermaid is startled, perplexed, and confused. But she knows they cannot go back. The New Desert is their Home. She remembers what Grand Mother Yemaya Mermaid says: "Look to Nature. All answers can be found in that which is naturally wild."

And so once the Old Ems step out of the wash upon their arrival in the New Desert, Sister Bea Wilder Mermaid sets out to find the flow and rhythms of the New Desert.

At first, all seems chaotic. It is so different from what she has known. But she stands her ground, she breathes deeply, and she waits.

In a moment, an hour, a day, a year, a thousand years, she sees, hears, feels, tastes the new world. At first, nights and mornings are cool and the days are warmer. The prickly things grow beautifully-colored flowers. Shrubs blossom. Flowers grow up from the hard desert floor: often golden yellow but sometimes red or purple or white. Small owls stand in saguaro cavities making a strange squeaking noise. And other birds are everywhere hatching other birds. Sister Bea Wilder Mermaid is glad to make all of their acquaintances.

Then she begins seeing bobcats and coyotes walking the desert with their children. She introduces herself, but they often do not seem to know or understand her, and they continue on their way.

The days grow hotter. The wind usually arrives from the west when it comes. Flowers disappear.

Lizards appear. Snakes with rattles on the end of their tails slither around the New Desert. They move like Old Mermaids did in the Old Sea. Sister Bea Wilder Mermaid nods respectfully each time she encounters one and then steps out of the way.

She soon discovers the dry wash is cooler than the rest of the desert, especially if she finds a spot between mesquite trees. Sometimes she just stands wherever she is and lets the silence throb around her. At night, under a full moon, she watches mice with wings swoop down to the tall people-like cacti.

The days pulse with heat, and the nights are little different, except dark. One day the wind shifts. It comes from the south. She feels a strange pressure in the air. Soon it begins to rain. It is as if the entire Old Sea is being dropped on the desert. Flowers bloom again. Javelinas gorge on the fruit of the prickly trees. Baby lizards run everywhere. The prickly trees swell after the rains. Birds and butterflies fill the skies.

And then the wind shifts again. The heat returns. When Sister Bea Wilder Mermaid thinks she cannot bear the heat, it begins to cool slightly, and then more dramatically. Small birds with whirring wings and long bills are everywhere. The world becomes golden in many places.

Life moves faster and cooler. The world feels relaxed and playful. At night sometimes it is so cold it hurts. Jackrabbits graze everywhere, finding goodies on the desert floor.

It begins to warm up. The wildflowers bloom, and the desert is yellow and purple in spots. The birds begin mating and laying eggs again.

Sister Bea Wilder Mermaid takes a breath, closes and opens her eyes. She looks behind her where the Old Mermaids wait. She can tell them now if the heat becomes too much to bear, just wait. The rain will come. If the rain fills the washes and threatens to flood the world, she can say, just wait. The heat will come again. And then the cool. And then the flowers. And the babies. And the heat. No chaos here. Just the wild and the wild things.

Spring
Sister Bea Wilder Mermaid

Wisdom: Embrace wild beautiful prickliness.

This is a photo of the small prickly pear cactus (Opuntia microdasys). Microdasys means small and hairy. Its common Anglo name is bunny ears or angel's wings. This tiny opuntia is often hidden amongst other desert flora and is only noticeable for a short time in the spring when its tiny blossoms open up.

If you're ever near them, pay attention to the "hairy" part. Instead of thorns, they have glochids which look like harmless bits of hair, but they are barbed, difficult to remove, and can be irritating—figuratively and literally.

I don't know for sure, but I believe . . . the Old Mermaids love this little prickly pear. It often pops up in areas where pack rats have built nests and destroyed bigger prickly pears. Somehow this tiny cactus survives, opening up a few blossoms in the spring, the flowers like dinner table presents for the pack rats or anyone else who is paying attention.

Sister Bea Wilder Mermaid was convinced that cottontails shape-shifted into these prickly pears every once in a while when they just wanted to get away from it all.

When she told Sister Laughs A Lot Mermaid about this, Sister Laughs A Lot Mermaid said, "I have seen some amazing things here since we washed ashore, but I've never seen a rabbit become a cactus. Could it be?"

"It's just in this one spot," Sister Bea Wilder Mermaid said. "On the other side of the fence." She pointed. "See where the pack rat house is and next to it is that big nopal that is melting into the ground? See the small bunny ears next to all of that?"

Sister Laughs A Lot Mermaid nodded. "But I see no bunnies. Although I suppose the pads look vaguely like bunny ears."

"Just wait."

"Why would a bunny want to be a cactus?"

"Bunnies are so soft," Sister Bea Wilder Mermaid said. "I bet sometimes they just want to be prickly."

Not too long after that, the sister mermaids saw three rabbits running across the desert, chasing one another. Every once in a while the rabbits would turn around, and the one who was being chased began chasing. They did this several times. And then suddenly they ran toward the fence. The smallest bunny leaped through the space between the boards on the fence and was gone. The other two rabbits stood at the fence watching.

Sister Bea Wilder Mermaid and Sister Laughs A Lot Mermaid hurried over to the fence and stood next to the bunnies. They looked down at the opuntia microdasys. No rabbit was in sight.

"Where did it go?" Sister Laughs A Lot Mermaid asked.

Sister Bea Wilder Mermaid pointed to a bunny ears cactus with two small peach-colored blossoms on each bunny ear. "I bet that's the rabbit."

Just then, the other two rabbits began running away. The Old Ems turned to watch them. A moment later, the third rabbit emerged from under the fence and began chasing the other two again. Sister Bea Wilder Mermaid quickly looked back at the bunny ears cactus. The cactus with the peach-colored blossoms was still there.

"Perhaps I was wrong about that," Sister Bea Wilder Mermaid said.

Sister Laughs A Lot Mermaid leaned over and picked up something from the dirt and held it up for Sister Bea Wilder Mermaid to see. It was a small peach-colored petal.

"The last little rabbit dropped it," she said.

Sister Bea Wilder Mermaid laughed. "I guess we'll never know."

"Sometimes it is best to let the mystery be," Sister Laughs A Lot Mermaid said.

The Old Ems locked arms and ran after the three bunnies to see what they could see.

Meanings: Prickly beauty. It's best not to romanticize nature. It is red in tooth and claw as well as beautiful and ugly and amazing. Sometimes you can be a part of the wild by observing. Sometimes we dig deeper, and sometimes it is best to let the wild thing be, along with the mystery.

Dry Summer
Sister Bea Wilder Mermaid
Wisdom: **Embrace the wild things and leave them alone.**

This is a fan palm tree in the Old Mermaids Sanctuary with a male hooded oriole looking out from it.

When we first started coming to the Sanctuary, when it was Endicott West, owls roosted in the palm tree during the day. Now the owls stay in the pine tree when they visit, and a pair of hooded orioles take over part of the palm tree for part of the year. They are gorgeous brightly-colored additions to the Old Mermaids Sanctuary, especially when it is so hot and dry that it's difficult to believe bright colors still exist.

Hooded orioles are members of the blackbird family. In this part of the world, they often nest in fan palm trees and are sometimes called palm tree orioles. They strip fibers from the bottom of palm leaves and then weave these fibers up through another palm leaf to create an incredible pouch-like hanging nest. The female does most of the sewing. The male helps gather materials when needed, the female sits on the eggs she lays until they hatch, and both parents take care of the young birds.

The orioles don't hang around the Sanctuary all year round, preferring the tropics during the cooler winter months. But when they are here, their songs are beautiful and persistent, and the flashes of orange-yellow and black against the sky as the male flies quickly from tree to tree are astonishingly beautiful.

Sister Bea Wilder Mermaid enjoyed the orioles for

their ability to make home where they are, near people or away from them. She loved looking up at the palm tree and watching the birds live their lives high above them.

I don't know for certain, but I believe . . . one summer the Old Mermaids heard rumors about the nests of the hooded orioles. Someone somewhere was telling the tale that a flock of orioles had been seen at the house of an old witch who was unraveling her most magic blanket and throwing the threads to the wind. This sometimes occurred, the Old Ems were told, when a magical person was coming to the end of her or his days. They needed to unwind some magic safely before they made their way through the veils.

This time, so the rumor went, the orioles had taken the threads that were still full of magic and woven those threads into their hanging nests. Now those nests were worth more than gold, diamonds, or emeralds: If someone got a hold of one of the nests, their every wish would be fulfilled.

Ah, what a tale!

When the Witch of Coyote Hill heard this, she told the Old Mermaids and the Old Neighbors that it was nonsense.

"For one thing, no witch I know is dying any time soon. For another thing, if our blankets had threads that allowed us to fulfill our every desire, don't you think we'd be unravelling them long before we took the long walk?"

Yet lo and behold, a young man who called himself KayCee came to the Old Mermaids Sanctuary looking for orioles.

"I heard you have a nest up in the palm tree," KayCee said. "I would like to look at it."

The Old Mermaids glanced at one another. Grand Mother Yemaya Mermaid nodded to Sister Bea Wilder Mermaid. The other Old Ems went about their business as Sister Bea Wilder Mermaid approached the young man and pointed to the palm.

"There it is," she said. "Our palm tree. But you can't see a nest from here, if there is one. I've never seen it." This was true. She had not seen their nest.

"That's what everyone says, but I think everyone is trying to keep me from the magical threads. I deserve them. You wouldn't believe the life I've had. I need a break. Those threads will give me everything I deserve."

"I am sorry you are having a tough life," Sister Bea Wilder Mermaid said. "However, if there is a nest, it belongs to the wild, not to you. The birds don't try to find threads in your house. So why would you try to find magic threads in theirs?"

"I told you why," he said. "I deserve it. Besides,

they are just birds. What do they contribute to the world?"

"Beauty, song, wildness."

The young man made a noise. "That is nothing. I am a human being. I contribute much more."

"Like what?" Sister Bea Wilder Mermaid asked.

"I *will* contribute a great deal, once I get those threads."

Sister Bea Wilder Mermaid reached down to the edge of her skirt and found a loose thread. She pulled on it, broke it, and held it out to KayCee. "This is a thread from my skirt," she said. "I'm sure it has just as much magic as the threads in that nest."

He shook his head. "I do not want *that*. If you don't let me climb up this palm tree. I will find another and get an oriole pouch."

"Look," Sister Bea Wilder Mermaid said, "I'm not supposed to tell anyone this." She figured if someone could make up a story about magical threads, so could she. "You are not the first person who has come looking for magical threads in the oriole nest. We let the others climb the tree, even helped them with the ladder, but they all disappeared once they climbed the ladder."

"What do you mean?"

Sister Bea Wilder Mermaid shrugged. "Anyone can see that the orioles are part fairy. You never try to steal from a fairy. You especially don't want to mess with their homes or children, and oriole children live in the pouches. Those people we let climb into the palm tree? We have never seen them again. They could all be in Summerland for all we know. Or somewhere worse. I'm only trying to protect you."

"I don't believe you," he said.

And he turned and walked away from Sister Bea Wilder Mermaid and the palm tree. She watched him walk into the desert and laughed. Where did this person come from? She did not want to see any more like him. It seemed as though he had lost his ability to understand the true value of anything.

As time went on, the Old Mermaids heard that KayCee did try climbing a neighbor's palm tree where an oriole couple apparently had a nest. The neighbor said KayCee went up the ladder, the neighbor turned away for a second, and when he looked back, KayCee was gone.

As far as anyone knows, KayCee was never seen again.

Meanings: Home can be anywhere, but don't try to steal anyone else's peace, quiet, or home. Especially in the dry summer when everyone is trying to survive. Nature does not owe you a thing. Honor the wild in the world and in yourself.

Monsoon
Sister Bea Wilder Mermaid
Wisdom: Follow the wild onto the Mystic Trail

The first time I saw a bobcat was at the Sanctuary a few days after I had finished writing *Church of the Old Mermaids*. I was walking around the Sanctuary, looking for some kind of vision or sign, as I contemplated leaving and going back home. Then I saw a bobcat, only I didn't know what she was. For a split second, I thought, "So this is what a fairy looks like."

This is how I described it in *Under the Tucson Moon*:

"I walked a few steps, toward a picnic table. The golden light from the setting sun fell beneath the palo verde and mesquite that grew side by side near the front of the house, fell like a kind of twilight spotlight, or a wave of sweet light—that kind of light where you're certain anything can happen.

"As I gazed at the place beneath the tree, something turned to me and opened her eyes. The sun had set in her eyes, golden red, split in two. She blinked and came into form. At first I thought she was a coyote. But her gaze was different. More fey. More direct. And her ears had tufts. Her face was rounder. I couldn't place what I was looking at. I put my hands together at my heart. 'Oh,' I said. And something else. Maybe, 'stay'? I can't remember. She stood, sleepy, and I saw her whole body. I knew the form now. Saw her short tail. Bobcat. She was smaller than what I would have imagined. She walked away slowly, down into the wash and across, up into the desert. She looked back at me once. Then she was gone.

"I looked for her. Looked for her prints in the old mermaid dust. It was enough that I had seen her. Enough that she sat under the trees, next to the bench, close to the house. Enough that I asked for a vision, and she let me see her."

The bobcat was real and wild. At the same time, she seemed to be inviting me to come with her into another world. And that's what the time of the monsoon is like: Other worlds open to us. The bobcat is wild. She is inviting us into the wild. Yet she will continue on with or without us. She is her own amazing wild being. The question for this card is: will you join her?

Meanings: Wild. What is it like to look the wild in the eyes and know she is looking back at you? Don't turn away. No matter how much you have been domesticated, part of you is wild, too.

Fall

Sister Bea Wilder Mermaid

Wisdom: Embrace the wildness in you.

Desert cottontail rabbits are ubiquitous in the Sonoran Desert and are a food source for just about every predator, including humans. Consequently, very few live to the ripe old age of two.

On the Sanctuary, the rabbits are a near constant source of joy and wonder for us as they play or fight and chase each other, often in the old horse corrals that we now call the Rabbit Corrals.

In the dry hot summer months, they will often make "forms" in our flower beds in the relatively-cool sand there, and sleep for most of the day. The rabbits create these forms by digging out shallow indentations in the dirt. They allow other rabbits and sometimes birds to share the forms on occasion.

Desert rabbit ears are bigger than cottontails from other parts of the country. These big ears help them cool off better during those hot summer days. We see lots of ear injuries, although none quite as startling as what happened to Three Ears who showed up on our porch one evening with what looked like three ears.

The damage to the ear had healed long ago and

seemed not to affect the rabbit in any way we could discern. We were told these kinds of injuries to rabbits often came from birds of prey trying to grab the animal. Perhaps the bird picked Three Ears up by the ear, and the rabbit just slipped through the sharp talon as the ear ripped open.

The Old Mermaids had their own Three Ears, only it came to them as a baby, right after a hawk tried to carry it up into the sky. Three Ears hid in the Old Mermaids' garden for several days, until the ear healed. Well, the ear stopped bleeding, but now the ear was in two pieces so it looked like the rabbit had three ears.

And something peculiar happened. Three Ears's hearing seemed to suddenly improve. She was always listening intently to some thing. If what she was listening to turned out to be something harmless, she would continue eating. If it was something potentially harmful, she would keep listening while backing into a corner or running under the skirts of one of the Old Ems and staying there until the danger passed.

Sometimes the danger was something that could hurt the rabbit, but sometimes it was danger that could hurt the Old Mermaids and their neighbors, like the time a hailstorm passed over them. Or the time Bad Bart came looking for someone to fight with. Grand Mother Yemaya Mermaid sent him on his way by giving him directions to a town over the mountains where

Bad Bart's nemesis Copper Gary had fled. Or so she said. There actually was no town over the mountain that way, only a lot of rattlesnakes and no one named Copper Gary.

Then the little girl Stari came to visit her cousin who was one of the neighbors to the Old Mermaids. Stari's father had recently disappeared, and now she and her mother were wandering the land looking for home or answers or the father. Stari noticed right away that Three Ears could hear danger before it arrived. And she began spending as much time with the rabbit as possible.

"It's a wild animal," Sister Bea Wilder Mermaid told her, "so we leave her be."

"I can't touch her?"

"It's better for her if we leave her wild," Sister Bea Wilder Mermaid said.

"But I could take care of her, and she could keep me safe."

Sister Bea Wilder Mermaid said, "Why don't you just watch her from afar?"

And so she did. Whenever Three Ears ran to hide, Stari did the same—although she did not try to hide under the skirts of any Old Mermaid. Instead, she would run into her mother's arms or into the Old Mermaids' house.

After a while, Sister Bea Wilder Mermaid could

see that Stari was not feeling safer. She was becoming more nervous, more like a rabbit than a little girl. Stari's mother told Sister Bea Wilder Mermaid that the girl was hardly sleeping or eating, and she was constantly worried that her mother was going to disappear, too.

One day Stari and Sister Bea Wilder Mermaid sat on the edge of the pool with their legs dangling in the water. Three Ears was grazing on a patch of desert grass under a small creosote bush nearby.

"You know the reason Three Ears has three ears is because a bird tried to eat her," Sister Bea Wilder Mermaid said.

Stari nodded. "That would be terrible to be eaten by a bird. Or by anything, really."

Sister Bea Wilder Mermaid agreed. "Lots of animals eat rabbits. Because they are prey for so many predators, they have to be on the alert much of the time. Just like Three Ears is. But you've noticed Three Ears still plays with the other rabbits. She still sleeps, she eats, she has a good life."

Stari watched the rabbit. "Where do you think her parents are?"

Sister Bea Wilder Mermaid glanced at the rabbit. "They probably got eaten."

Stari's eyes widened. "Really? That's terrible!"

"Everybody's gotta eat," Sister Bea Wilder Mermaid said. "It's part of nature. When we die, bugs and bacteria and other things will eat our bodies. We will be a part of nature always."

Stari frowned. Sister Bea Wilder Mermaid could tell she was not reassuring the girl.

"We aren't rabbits," Sister Bea Wilder Mermaid said. "We don't have as much to worry about as they do. No bird is going to try to eat us."

"Are you sure?" Stari asked. "Birds gotta eat."

Sister Bea Wilder Mermaid laughed. "That's true. I am sure no bird is going to eat you while you are alive. No coyote or bobcat is going to eat us either."

"Are you sure?"

"I am sure," Sister Bea Wilder Mermaid said. "Bad things happen, love. And good things happen, too. Look where you are."

"On the Old Mermaids Sanctuary," Stari said as she looked around. "Where magic happens."

"Magic happens everywhere," Sister Bea Wilder Mermaid said. "And even hurt, we can still thrive."

"Even if we can't hear danger coming?" Stari asked.

"Even if," Sister Bea Wilder Mermaid said. "And I'm not sure Three Ears can hear it coming either. I think she just likes hiding under the skirts of the Old Mermaids."

Stari laughed. "I bet." She sighed. "OK. I am hungry."

"What would you like to eat?" Sister Bea Wilder Mermaid asked. "I'll make it for you."

"Rabbit stew," Stari said. She looked at the Old Mermaid and grinned. Sister Bea Wilder Mermaid laughed.

"Humans gotta eat," Stari said, grinning.

And so they do.

Meanings: No matter what is going on in your life, thrive. You don't want to only survive; you want to thrive. Bad things happen, but so do good things. And you've gotta sleep and eat and find joy now and again. Chop wood, carry water, and laugh.

Winter
Sister Bea Wilder Mermaid
Wisdom: **Embrace wild protection.**

This small cactus is part of the Mammillaria genus—which means nipple in Latin—and we call these small cacti around the Sanctuary pin cushion. Other mammillaria are also called pin cushion and globe, nipple, and birthday cake cactus.

These small cacti are usually found half-hidden beneath other cacti or snuggled up close to a log as it is here in this card. This is probably a mesquite tree bone. This cactus is growing up in a kind of charnel ground, so to speak, a graveyard out in the open. The mesquite tree died—or part of it died—and from those bones the seeds of this cactus took refuge, sprouted, and grew.

Meanings: In the Sonoran Desert, winter can be more of a social time than it is the rest of the year, but you may be inclined to rest and relax. In any case, protect yourself. Know that you can be protected by the bones of the ancestors and still grow into a whole and thriving person. Hunker down with the wild. It's time.

Sister Lyra Musica Mermaid

Suggestion: **Fear has no sisters, but I have many.**

Mystery: **Live your siren song.**

Sister Lyra Musica Mermaid had a difficult time when the Old Mermaids got to the New Desert. She missed the Old Sea, and she was afraid much of the time in this new world. Things got better once she confronted the Hunter (in *Church of the Old Mermaids*), but she still had problems occasionally. Like many of us, she had to work to keep from being too fearful or anxious. Her life was a journey to discover her siren song and then to keep singing it. **Whenever you get her cards, whatever season, she is urging you to move beyond your fears to find and then "sing" your siren song, whatever it might be.**

Spring
Sister Lyra Musica Mermaid
Wisdom: Sing your siren song.

The cactus wren is a tough little bird, bigger than most other wrens. It is ubiquitous in the Sonoran desert, yet habitat destruction is taking its toll. Cactus wrens are curious and often loud birds, rambunctious and seemingly fearless. Obviously, given their name, they do like cacti. On this card, the cactus wren is perched on the sacred saguaro—the sentinel of the Sonoran Desert—and it is singing its song.

I don't know for sure, but I believe . . . Sister Lyra Musica Mermaid was walking the wash and feeling as though she were filled up with anxiety and nothing else when she heard: "Hey, quit interrupting my song."

Sister Lyra Musica Mermaid looked around. She didn't see anyone who would understand her language. A cactus wren on top of a short saguaro was watching her.

"Yes, you," Cactus Wren said.

"I'm sorry," Sister Lyra Musica Mermaid said, "but I wasn't saying anything. How could I be interrupting your song?"

"Your thoughts, baby," Cactus Wren said. "Your

entire vibe. Why are you so afraid? Look at me: I am literally standing on pins."

"You are literally standing on cactus needles."

"Pins, needles, what's the difference? You don't see me whining about it. Or being afraid of it. And see that hawk circling up there? It wants to end me dead, but I am gonna sing my song if it kills me."

Sister Lyra Musica Mermaid looked up. "And it might kill you. Why don't you hide until it's gone?"

"I might do that," Cactus Wren said. "And some days I do that. But today the sky is blue, these needles are sharp, and I want to sing my song."

"The hawk is gone," Sister Lyra Musica Mermaid said.

"There's always something else who wants to eat us," it said.

"How do you stand on those needles?"

"Very carefully," Cactus Wren said. "How do you walk on those legs?"

"Very carefully," Sister Lyra Musica Mermaid said. "So you know who we are. And who we were."

"Of course," Cactus Wren said. "Everyone knows. And, baby, we were all something else at one time."

Sister Lyra Musica Mermaid nodded. "That doesn't help me not be afraid."

Cactus Wren nodded. "Sometimes I am so afraid I shake in my boots."

Sister Lyra Musica Mermaid cocked her head, trying to imagine the cactus wren in boots.

"Metaphorically speaking," Cactus Wren said.

"What do you do when you are afraid?" Sister Lyra Musica Mermaid asked.

"I think of fear and anxiety as background noise," Cactus Wren said. "A kind of white noise that sometimes fills the Universe." The bird shrugged. "And then I sing. I mean, what else?"

"What else, indeed."

Cactus Wren opened its beak wide and said, "Top of the world, Ma!"

"Bottom of the world, Ma!" Sister Lyra Musica Mermaid said from her place in the wash.

"OK, OK, leave the singing to the professionals," Cactus Wren said.

"Really?"

"No, sing away. But sing away from here. I'm trying to find love. Nothing personal, but you're not my type."

Sister Lyra Musica Mermaid laughed. "I love you anyway. And I'm going to sing about it all day. Away, far away from here."

The Old Em continued down the wash, with the cactus wren's song at her back and her own song at her front.

Meanings: Perhaps your fears are stopping you. It's

time to let them go. Easier said than done. But some days you can sing them away or let another creature sing them away for you. They may return; in the meantime, sing your siren song—or go looking for it.

Dry Summer
Sister Lyra Musica Mermaid
Wisdom: Dance your siren song.

These are the blooms of cereus cactus, also known as Night Blooming Cactus or Queen of the Night Cactus. For most of the year, this cactus looks like a stick in the ground. In the last weeks of May or at the beginning of June, they get fuzzy bumps that eventually blossom into fluorescent white flowers that only last for a day or less. The cactus is able to hold these big flowers up because a huge tuber grows from the bottom of it (and is beneath the surface).

The Old Ems first saw the big white flowers one night when Sister Magdelene Mermaid needed help finding her way home in the dark. The flowers acted as lanterns leading her home. (The name cereus means "torch" or "candle.") Every year, it seemed, one or more of the Old Mermaids would have an adventure on the one night that the Queens of the Night blossomed.

One year, Sister Lyra Musica Mermaid was out

walking in the desert. As often happens when faeries are afoot—even when one might be a-faery—Sister Lyra Musica Mermaid got separated from the other Old Mermaids. She was left alone in the dark. In the desert. In the time of year when the rattlesnakes were out. And the mountain lions. Coyotes. She was an Old Mermaid. She didn't worry about such things. Except when she did.

Before this new life, she could have dived deep into the ocean and gotten away from any danger. At least, that was what she believed. Now she often felt herself sinking inward—almost as though she was getting smaller—so that nothing could touch her or hurt her again. Or maybe her heart was getting smaller because she didn't think she could take one more heartache.

Then suddenly on this night, a woman in white was walking toward her in the desert. It wasn't that she was wearing white. It was as if she were a beautiful flower with a light at her center that made her a human-like lantern.

"Hello, Sister Lyra," the flower woman said as she held out her hand to Sister Lyra Musica Mermaid.

"Hello, Queen of the Night," the Old Mermaid said, taking the woman's hand in hers. "You have come to light my way home like you did with Sister Magdelene Mermaid?"

The Queen of the Night smiled. She led Sister Lyra Musica Mermaid around the pencil cholla, the teddy bear cholla, the mesquite trees, and creosote bushes to a clearing in the desert where several other Queens of the Night were dancing. They all looked different from each other yet were the same, too, dancing under the stars.

"Shall we dance?" the Queen of the Night asked Sister Lyra.

Sister Lyra Musica Mermaid smiled. "Of course."

And so Sister Lyra Musica Mermaid danced with this Queen and then all of the Queens of the Night until her feet were sore and the sky began to lighten.

"This was so much fun," Sister Lyra Musica Mermaid said. "I can't wait to do it again. I will miss you all so. Shall we meet next year at the same time?"

The Queen smiled. "You long for what was and you fear what will be."

"I want to always be this happy," Sister Lyra Musica Mermaid said.

The Queen laughed. "This here and now is what we have."

Sister Lyra Musica Mermaid smiled. "I know it's best to live in the present. But it was so awful when we lost the Old Sea. I miss it so much sometimes that it hurts."

"Then miss it," the Queen said. "And let it hurt.

That will subside. Or it won't. Things are not always easy. Yet beauty is lurking around somewhere most of the time. Open your heart to it all."

Sister Lyra Musica Mermaid closed her eyes for a moment and breathed deeply. Then she nodded, opened her eyes, and said, "I will do just that."

The other queens came and hugged and kissed Sister Lyra Musica Mermaid. Then they drifted away until all their lights were out of sight. Just then the Sun began to rise, and golden light streamed across the desert. Sister Lyra Musica Mermaid watched it for a time, and then she hurried home to the Old Mermaids Sanctuary.

Meanings: Life isn't always easy. Don't despair. Find beauty, especially in your own siren song. Open your heart to the world. And if a flower offers to dance with you, accept.

Monsoon
Sister Lyra Musica Mermaid
Wisdom: Center yourself in your home.

Sometimes the best way to get centered and to sing our siren songs is to create home. We can do this with the songs or chants we sing when putting it all together. This is a mystical time of the year. It's an excellent time to look at our living space and see if it is really a home.

The Old Mermaids felt more at home in the New Desert once they built their house.

They used mud, straw, stone, and water—all materials from the old dried sea. As they built the house, they let the mud and straw and stone tell them stories. They listened to what the cacti and coyotes and crows had to say, too.

The neighbors had more stories, which made the work easier, and the house liked the tales, too. It shaped itself beautifully around them and this land. It was a piece of art.

They painted scenes from the Old Sea on the walls. And scenes from the mountains. Valleys. The desert. These paintings on the walls were so realistic that you would swear you could walk right into them and keep on going.

Everyone liked to be invited to the Old Mermaids Sanctuary because it was so beautiful. Many people—even to this day—swear the house was alive.

When they finished the house, Sister Lyra Musica Mermaid said to Grand Mother Yemaya Mermaid, "I feel more at home now."

Grand Mother Yemaya Mermaid nodded. "Sometimes it is not enough to wish for home. Sometimes we have to actually build it and then practice being at home in it.

That's exactly what Sister Lyra Musica Mermaid did: She practiced being at home in the New Desert until it felt like home.

Meanings: It might be time to build your home, literally or metaphorically. Perhaps you need to shake things up in your living spaces and make them holier or more yours. Maybe you just need to feel the earth between your fingers.

Fall

Sister Lyra Musica Mermaid

Wisdom: **Create or find a room of your own.**

The Quail House is a tiny writing/art studio on the Sanctuary. It was unpainted for a long time, and it blended in perfectly with the surrounding Sonoran Desert. Many artists and writers have used this building over the years. I wrote *Church of the Old Mermaids* and *The Fish Wife* here, along with many other books.

Recently, age, the drought, and the unrelenting heat took a toll on the building, so Mario and I shored it up, did some repairs, and painted it. We wanted Southwest colors, and I was inspired by Frida Kahlo's color palette of her home in Mexico City.

We had often felt like visitors here because of the rich storied history of the place. Fixing up the Quail House also made it ours.

The Old Mermaids had writing and art studios, too. When Sister Lyra Musica Mermaid decided she wanted to do some writing and drawing, she took over their Quail House for a while. She replaced old boards, put in new nails where needed, and redecorated the entire thing.

Sissy Maggie was so talented at painting and designing; Sister Ruby Rosarita was an amazing chef; Sisters Faye and Bridget Mermaid came up with the most inventive chants. So at first Sister Lyra Musica Mermaid felt a bit intimidated trying something creative. She could never be as good as they were. But then she painted the Quail House, she moved things around, she sang her own songs, and the place became hers for a time.

As you know, Sister Lyra Musica Mermaid had a bit of trouble when the Old Mermaids first washed up onto the shores of the New Desert. The New World was a little bit too new for her. She worked to understand the rhythms and ways of the desert, just as all the Old Ems did. But Sister Lyra Musica Mermaid was accustomed to harmony, and life in the New Desert was not always harmonious. She often felt uneasy, and this uneasiness made her uncomfortable. Sometimes she wandered the desert looking for something to ease the discomfort.

She walked the desert and listened to the trees. She listened to the thorny ones. She listened to the bushy ones. She heard their songs; she sensed their voices. She discovered when they dropped their leaves and when they grew their fruit. She knew which ones were full of water and which ones were not. Even during the hottest times of the year, she felt the harmony of the place.

She watched for and listened to the animals. She knew she could follow the fox and bobcat into myth. Coyotes brought her music, but she needed to keep her distance. Mountain Lion would follow her to and fro with harm to none, unless the lion decided she was hungry. The Rattler had stories to tell, but death could await at the end of such tales if Sister Lyra Musica Mermaid was not full of care. And no one could part the veils between here and there the way Jackrabbit could.

Still, even knowing all this, Sister Lyra Musica Mermaid felt a bit out of place and out of balance now and again.

One day while she was wandering, Sister Lyra Musica Mermaid saw another woman coming toward her. Her gait was erratic, and she held her hands up to her head. Sister Lyra Musica Mermaid stopped and called, "Are you well? Do you need assistance?"

The woman seemed to see her for the first time, even though she had been heading straight for her. Soon they were feet apart from one another.

"Are you lost?" Sister Lyra Musica Mermaid asked.

"I am indeed," the woman said. "My name is Dolores, and I've come to find my way. I have long heard of the Old Mermaids Sanctuary."

Sister Lyra Musica Mermaid smiled and said, "You are welcome, of course. I will take you to my sister mermaids."

They began to walk through the desert together.

"I have been searching my whole life to find a place where I belong," Dolores said. "I feel so lost most of the time."

"I hear you, sister," Sister Lyra Musica Mermaid said. "When we first arrived here, I was—"

"I bet you know everything about here," Dolores said. "And you can tell me. I want to be just like you."

Sister Lyra Musica Mermaid was startled. How could this woman decide she wanted to be just like her when she knew nothing about her?

"I can tell this is the place," Dolores said. "I know it. As soon as I saw you, I knew you were the answer. Look at you. You are so at home here."

"Well, when we first—"

"I bet if I had grown up in a place like this, I would know my way."

Dolores began telling Sister Lyra Musica Mermaid the story of her life. She had grown up in a place not like the New Desert and raised by parents who did not understand that she was a seeker who had no time for the trivia of their lives. Finally one day she left and was free of their influence. Dolores told her tale quickly—except when it came to some part of her life where someone had mistreated her. Then she slowed and told those stories with relish. Sister Lyra Musica Mermaid tried to take it all in, but truth to tell, she was relieved when they finally arrived at the "Welcome to the Old Mermaids Sanctuary" sign.

Sister Lyra Musica Mermaid opened the gate for Dolores and then led the way to the garden where Sisters Faye and Laughs A Lot Mermaid were working. The Old Ems rose from the dirt as Sister Lyra Musica Mermaid approached with Dolores.

"This is Dolores, and she has come to visit," Sister Lyra Musica Mermaid said.

"Welcome!" Sister Laughs A Lot Mermaid said. "We love having visitors."

"No, I am not a visitor," Dolores said. "I want to live here. I know this is my place. Oh, look at that dirt! And you planted all of this, and it's growing. That is profound." She took a deep breath. "Yes, I knew it. That is what I want to be. This is what I want to do. Please show me the way to be a great gardener."

Sister Faye Mermaid glanced at Sister Lyra Musica Mermaid who pressed her lips together and shrugged. Soon enough Dolores was down in the dirt with them.

Sister Lyra Musica Mermaid did not see Dolores again that day until dinner when all the Old Mermaids gathered round to partake in some of Sister Ruby Rosarita Mermaid's chili. It wasn't quite the famous chili that had more than once fed everyone on the Old Mermaids Sanctuary and beyond. It was her Better Than Average Chili which was made not only with Old Mermaids' tears but also with seaweed the Old Neighbors The Pepperman and The Pepperwoman had given them.

Dolores took one bite of the chili and said, "Oh my! This is the best chili I've ever had! I've had a revelation! An epiphany! I must become a chef! That is how I'll make my way in the world. Please, Sister Ruby Rosarita Mermaid, will you train me?"

Sister Ruby Rosarita Mermaid said, "Darlin', I am no chef. I can certainly teach you how to cook."

"Oh, what a gift!" Dolores said. "I knew I belonged here."

And so it went over the next few days. Everywhere

Dolores went, she was certain it was her place. She was certain she had found her life's work.

When they visited Annie Who Loves Birds, Dolores promised that birds would be her focus from now until the end of her time.

When Dolores went to the Tea Shell, she swore she would now dedicate her life to serving others tea and whatever else the Tea Shell served.

As a rule, the Old Ems were accepting of others. They didn't judge whether someone talked too much or too little. They didn't judge a person by the clothes she wore or the work she did. However, Sister Lyra Musica Mermaid was confused by Dolores. In fact, she admitted to herself that she did not like her.

Since Dolores arrived, Sister Lyra Musica Mermaid felt out of balance. The whole of the Old Mermaids Sanctuary was out of balance. She had brought Dolores into their lives, so it was up to her to remedy the situation. She asked for advice from Grand Mother Yemaya Mermaid who was standing next to a saguaro listening to a thrasher sing when she came upon her.

"It's Dolores," Sister Lyra Musica Mermaid said. "That is why nothing is harmonious anymore. She has put everything out of balance."

Grand Mother Yemaya Mermaid looked around and then said, "What is out of balance? The sun still rises and falls. The moon still rises and falls. The thrasher still sings. The air is clear. The water is clear. I see clarity and balance all around."

Sister Lyra Musica Mermaid started to say, "But—" and then she stopped and took a deep breath. She looked around, too. Grand Mother Yemaya Mermaid was right.

"She has only knocked me out of balance then," Sister Lyra Musica Mermaid said.

"Has she?" Grand Mother Yemaya Mermaid asked. "Are you out of balance?"

"I certainly feel off-balance," Sister Lyra Musica Mermaid said.

"But why?"

"She seems so desperate," Sister Lyra Musica Mermaid said, "and uncomfortable."

"What has that to do with you?" Grand Mother Yemaya Mermaid asked. "You aren't required to be with her."

"But I understand her," Sister Lyra Musica Mermaid said, "in a way. I understand her discomfort. I want her to be at ease."

"So that you will also be at ease?"

Sister Lyra Musica Mermaid hesitated, and then she said, "Yes, you're right."

It wasn't about Dolores. It was about her own unease in the world. She still did not feel as though she belonged. She had been seeking answers from all kinds of places, too, just as Dolores had.

Sister Lyra Musica Mermaid went and sat on the sandy bottom of the wash for a time. Her toes dug into the earth. She breathed. She listened to the world around her buzz slightly. She realized that it all looked and sounded and felt familiar. She supposed that was one definition of home: familiarity. She smiled. That was a step in the right direction.

Sister Lyra Musica Mermaid was late heading out to Flat Rock Woman where the Old Mermaids would sing up the Moon. Partway there, she heard a woman crying. She hurried toward the sound and found Dolores standing near an old palo verde tree, crying.

She looked up when Sister Lyra Musica Mermaid neared. "There's nothing to lean against here!" she said. "No tree that won't prick me to death. No people, to speak of!"

"It is indeed a thorny place," Sister Lyra Musica Mermaid said. "May I help you with something?"

"I keep trying things," she said, "but I still don't feel as though I have a place in the world. Can you tell me what to do?"

Sister Lyra Musica Mermaid said, "No, I can't tell you what to do. It seems like you see someone and then you try to do what they are doing and be who they are being. Why not be yourself?"

Dolores began sobbing. "There is no myself. I'm empty."

"Congratulations!" Sister Lyra Musica Mermaid said. "Sister Sophia Mermaid has said some humans spend their entire lives trying to be empty!"

Dolores chuckled. She wiped her eyes. "I think it's a different kind of empty."

"You just need to find your own voice," Sister Lyra Musica Mermaid said. "Sometimes we need to be still and quiet, and sometimes we can find our own voice with others."

Sister Lyra Musica Mermaid took Dolores's hand. "Come on! We'll sing up the moon."

Sister Lyra Musica Mermaid and Dolores got to Flat Rock Woman just before the Moon rose up over the mountains. The Old Mermaids and Dolores stood on the rock, barefoot. This night, they all chanted, "Ahhhhhhh!" and then "Ohhhhh!" and then they each chose their own wordless sound. Some of them danced and clapped, too. Sister Lyra Musica Mermaid felt as though everything was in balance once again as the Moon rose above the Mountains, encouraged by the voices of the women.

When they were finished chanting and then chatting, after the Moon came up and the women had been silent for a while, Sister Lyra Musica Mermaid asked Dolores, "How are you feeling now?"

Dolores smiled and said, "Full enough."

Sister Lyra Musica Mermaid nodded. "Me, too."

Meanings: Even in our own homes, sometimes we need a room of our own. We need spaces and places where we can be ourselves and not have to take care of anyone else or fix anyone else's problems. A lot of times that means we have to have the resources to have such a room, which is what Virginia Woolf was writing about in her essay *A Room of One's Own*. Women needed money and a room to write in. Figure out how to get your Quail House, your Room of One's Own, even if it turns out not to be a literal room.

Winter
Sister Lyra Musica Mermaid

Wisdom: **Stillness and quiet can be a siren song.**

Occasionally it snows on the Old Mermaids Sanctuary. This is a photo of one of those times, looking down the wash on the west side of the house. We see all kinds of wildlife in this wash: rabbits, bobcats, coyotes, javelinas, birds, snakes. When it snows like this, the Sanctuary is so quiet. Hardly any creatures are stirring. It's a wonderful time to take a breath, to take in the scenery, and just enjoy.

Meanings: Is there a chill in some part of your life? Is it something you need to fix or can you just breathe and let it go until the sun comes out again? Maybe it is a chill and stillness that you need.

Sister Laughs A Lot Mermaid

Suggestion: **She who laughs a lot laughs a lot.**

Mystery: **Cultivate joy.**

Sister Laughs A Lot Mermaid is a lot of fun. She has her ups and downs just like any being, but she does love to laugh. She finds joy wherever she goes, which has led her on an adventure or more. **Whenever you get one of her cards, it is an invitation to laugh and have a good time.**

One day she was walking through the desert on her way to visit The Pepperwoman and The Pepperman when she heard the tinkling of a tiny bell. She stopped and listened. She knew from her time in the Old Sea that the sound of a tiny bell like this could mean the Good Folk were about. Of course, to some, she and the Old Mermaids were part of the Good Folk—and maybe everything and everyone on the Old Mermaids

Sanctuary were part of that Other World. She didn't know. She didn't think about it. That would be too close to contemplating existence itself, and that was not Sister Laughs A Lot Mermaid's way. Instead, she walked toward the sound. As she walked, the sound stopped.

But soon enough she was at the lip of the wash. Across the way, she saw what appeared to be a human-sized jackrabbit, standing with its arms crossed, leaning against a saguaro. Sister Laughs A Lot Mermaid blinked and looked again. This time she saw a woman who appeared at first to be naked or covered in a light brown fur. When she blinked again, she saw the woman was wearing something that was very light brown—and her hair was all white. She had the biggest ears of almost anything Sister Laughs A Lot Mermaid had ever seen before, except, of course, for jackrabbits.

The woman moved away from the saguaro and motioned to the Old Mermaid. Sister Laughs A Lot Mermaid wondered how on Earth she could lean against a saguaro.

Sister Laughs A Lot Mermaid crossed the wash and walked toward the woman.

"Hello," Sister Laughs A Lot Mermaid said. "Welcome!"

"Welcome? What do you mean 'welcome' as if

this place is not already my home. Who are you to welcome me to my home?"

"I'm sorry!" Sister Laughs A Lot Mermaid said, startled. "I don't recognize you. I'm Sister Laughs A Lot Mermaid. I live with the other Old Mermaids in the Sanctuary."

"Hmph."

"I heard a bell tinkling so I came your way," Sister Laughs A Lot Mermaid said.

The woman uncrossed her arms and seemed to relax. "Ahhh! Then you are exactly who I need. I am Jack." The woman put out her left hand palm up, the way magical beings all over the world greet each other. Sister Laughs A Lot Mermaid placed her left hand over Jack's hand. They held hands for an instant and then turned their hands to shake like other people, only they were shaking with their left instead of their right.

"If you heard the bell, then perhaps you can lead me to it," Jack said. "I got separated from my drove. We had a bit of spat, I got angry, and I walked off, and I forgot who I am."

"Jackrabbits get angry?"

"Who said anything about jackrabbits? Can you help me or not?" She was cranky again.

"I don't hear the bell any more," Sister Laughs A

Lot Mermaid said, "but I'll do whatever I can to help you. Where did you last see your bell?"

"If I knew that, I wouldn't need you," Jack said.

Sister Laughs A Lot Mermaid laughed.

"That was not meant to be funny," Jack said.

"Nevertheless," Sister Laughs A Lot Mermaid said.

"I think I was in the dry river," Jack said, "although I can't be sure."

"What's the bell look like?" Sister Laughs A Lot Mermaid asked.

"You ask a lot of questions."

"Are two questions a lot?" Sister Laughs A Lot Mermaid asked.

Jack made a face. "It's small, silver, with a turquoise stone at the center of one side."

Sister Laughs A Lot Mermaid nodded. She listened again and heard nothing.

"I'm on my way to The Pepper's place," Sister Laughs A Lot Mermaid said. "They are great treasure hunters. They're right over the rise."

Jack looked around. "I don't want to forget where I was."

"We could put a big X on the ground to mark the spot," Sister Laughs A Lot Mermaid suggested.

Jack made a noise. "What? You think I'm a damn roadrunner?" She pulled up what she was wearing and pulled down something else she was wearing, and she promptly peed near the saguaro. "There," she said.

Sister Laughs A Lot Mermaid made an X with her heel, too.

And then Sister Laughs A Lot Mermaid led them over the rise and to The Pepper's place. The couple sat out front in the shade, fanning themselves, glasses of tea next to them.

"Welcome," The Pepperwoman said. "Sister Laughs A Lot Mermaid, you have brought a new friend."

"I am no friend," Jack said, "and I'm not new. Far from it. I remember this place before you or this building were here."

"Would you like some soup or tea?" The Pepperman asked.

"She's lost her bell," Sister Laughs A Lot Mermaid said.

The couple nodded. "We understand. You've lost your joy. Your reason for being. Your heart. Your compassion. We've heard that can happen."

The Pepperwoman and The Pepperman often surprised Sister Laughs A Lot Mermaid. They knew a lot more than one would think upon first meeting them.

Jack said, "Yes! I feel I am quite not myself, although I don't really remember. Have you heard bells this morning?"

"We have not," The Pepperwoman said, "but we will help you find it. Have some tea first, and we'll round up the others."

Jack accepted the tea, and The Pepperman went out and got neighbors from far and wide. Soon they were all wandering the desert looking and listening for a tiny bell.

"This reminds me of the time I lost my marbles," The Pepperman said. "It took us forever and a day to find them and The Pepperwoman says I'm still missing a few."

Everyone laughed. Except Jack. She looked at Sister Laughs A Lot Mermaid and asked, "Why is that funny?"

"It means he went crazy," Sister Laughs A Lot Mermaid said.

"That's not funny," Jack said.

"Nevertheless . . ."

"I feel crazy right now, and it's not funny!"

"He probably didn't really go crazy," Sister Laughs A Lot Mermaid said. "He was just joking."

They dodged rattlesnakes and thorns and each other's nerves. The sky was brilliant blue. The Old Ems joined the search, of course.

Sister Bridget Mermaid said to Sister Laughs A Lot Mermaid, "This sounds like someone else's magic. It's not always wise to interfere in such things."

"But she asked for help," Sister Laughs A Lot Mermaid said. "I didn't want to say no."

"I understand," Sister Bridget Mermaid said. "We'll just be on the lookout."

"To be sure."

And for a while longer, they wandered. One by one, they told a story or a joke. There was the one about the rattlesnake who lost her rattle but eventually found it where she'd last seen it (at the end of her tail), and she ended up joining a percussion band. Then the one where Old Coyote Woman decided to teach her grandpups about cooking, only everything kept coming out raw. And the Crow who fell in love with his reflection in a pool.

Jack did not laugh at any of it, although she smiled once or twice as the day wore on.

"I miss everything," Jack said. "Especially all those jackasses who made me mad."

Sister Laughs A Lot Mermaid laughed.

"I wasn't joking."

"But you said *jack*asses," Sister Laughs A Lot Mermaid said.

"It's not funny."

"Nevertheless . . ."

Eventually, neighbors began to fall away as they went back to their respective homes to nap or eat. The

Old Mermaids invited Jack to come back to the Sanctuary for a meal.

Jack said, "I am so amazed and appreciative that you all came out to help me. Thank you."

Jack continued to walk back toward where Sister Laughs A Lot Mermaid had first seen her. Suddenly Sister Laughs A Lot Mermaid heard the tinkling bell again.

"Did you hear that?" Sister Laughs A Lot Mermaid asked.

Jack said, "No."

Sister Laughs A Lot Mermaid looked down. They were standing right on the X marks the spot she had created with her heel earlier in the day. She looked across the way and saw eight huge jackrabbits. They were all standing on their hind legs with their arms in the air. Sister Laughs A Lot Mermaid pointed. Jack followed her gaze and saw the jackrabbits.

She began to laugh. "Look at them! Grown jackrabbits acting like humans. How silly!" She laughed and laughed. Sister Laughs A Lot Mermaid laughed right along with her. The desert was filled with laughter.

Then she heard the bell again. She turned and looked at the mesquite tree next to her. There she saw a tiny silver bell hanging by a thread on one of the slender branches. She reached for it and took it from the tree.

"Look what I found," Sister Laughs A Lot Mermaid said. She handed the bell to Jack. The other eight jackrabbits were on their haunches now and no longer looked as big as a human person.

Jack held the bell between her forefinger and thumb and shook it slightly. The sound was pure joy. Jack pressed the tiny bell against her chest and then at her throat and finally on her forehead.

Then she held it out to Sister Laughs A Lot Mermaid. "Here. It's yours now. It's part of me. It always has been. I should've remembered that. It will bring you joy, always."

Sister Laughs A Lot Mermaid took the bell. Jack held out her left hand again, palm up, the way magical beings greet one another. Sister Laughs A Lot Mermaid placed her left hand over Jack's, held it for a moment, and they shook hands.

Then Jack was gone. She ran toward the jackrabbits, into dusk. Soon enough Sister Laughs A Lot Mermaid could no longer see her, could barely see the nine jackrabbits hopping away, springing through the near night toward who knows where.

Sister Laughs A Lot Mermaid took the bell back to the Sanctuary and told the Old Ems all about it. She put it on a string. If anyone ever forgot to laugh or was feeling joyless, Sister Laughs A Lot Mermaid gave them the bell to remind them.

It always worked.

Spring
Sister Laughs A Lot Mermaid
Wisdom: **Laugh a lot.**

We were surprised the first time we saw wild turkeys up in a canyon in the Santa Rita Mountains. We heard them first. It sounded like a human was walking through dry leaves. Then, through the trees, we spied what we thought were human beings coming our way. The flashy colors could only be human clothes. And then, we turned a corner or the colorful beings turned a corner or space and time switched places, and we saw they were not human beings—at least not any longer—they were wild turkeys. The males were all puffed out, showing off their feathery finery, trying to get the attention of the females, apparently; it seemed as though the other males were the only ones paying attention.

They looked like a family or a group of friends all decked out to go on a Sunday picnic, sitting under the sycamores along the dry creek.

I don't know for sure . . . but I believe Sister Laughs A Lot Mermaid was the first Old Em to stumble upon the wild turkeys. When she first saw them, she thought they were giants, at least giants as far as birds go. They were in a group under several Old Sycamore trees. Each turkey person was dressed in dark colorful clothes. Or feathers. Sister Laughs A Lot Mermaid couldn't tell which. She laughed and clapped her hands and was ready for adventure.

A big Ole Turkey Tom walked up to the Old Em. He puffed up his feathers at her.

"Would you care to walk on the wild side with me?" he asked, spreading his tail feathers up and behind him. He sure was pretty.

"What exactly would that entail?" she asked.

Ole Turkey Tom laughed. "I get it," he said. "That's funny as hell. En-tail. My tail is swell."

"Your tail is swell?"

"I need to *tell* the others."

Soon the Turkey People had gathered around her. They took turns telling jokes and puffing out their tails. Sister Laughs A Lot Mermaid did not always understand their jokes, but she laughed anyway. Jenny Wild Turkey kept saying to the males, "Stop doing that. She's an Old Em. She's not interested in your bones or feathers."

Ole Turkey Tom invited all the Old Mermaids for a feast under the sycamores. Sister Laughs A Lot Mermaid accepted on their behalf and ran back to camp to tell the Old Ems.

The Old Mermaids spent some time trying to figure out what to bring to the feast.

"Are they people or turkeys?" Sister Sophia Mermaid asked. "Are they faery and flighty? It's difficult to know."

They had brought nuts with them on their trip to the canyon, so they decided they would offer nuts. They dressed in whatever finery they had and soon walked to where the Old Wild Turkeys were awaiting them.

The Old Ems walked into the sycamore woods and were amazed to see a long table laden with food awaiting them. Sister Laughs A Lot Mermaid couldn't tell right away what the food was because Ole Tom Turkey and the others gathered around them. The Turkey Women put feathers in the Old Ems' hair, and the Turkey Men puffed out their chests and fanned their tail feathers.

Grand Mother Yemaya Mermaid held out their bowl of various nuts. "We hope this is enough for your splendid feast."

Ole Tom Turkey took the bowl and put it on the table.

"Thank you," Ole Tom Turkey said. "We appreciate it, but we have plenty. For our main dish, we always carve up a little mermaid."

"You carve up a little mermaid?" Sister Laughs A Lot Mermaid asked, momentarily alarmed.

Ole Tom Turkey laughed. "We always serve up a little lemonade." He slapped Sister Laughs A Lot Mermaid on the back. "You are a funny Old Mermaid."

"So I've been told," she said.

"You are very *old*?" he asked.

Jenny Wild Turkey opened her arms and said, "Let us break bread before this old turkey tries to make another joke."

And so they feasted on nuts and fruits and seeds and cakes. They all told jokes, and half of them the Old Mermaids didn't understand. It didn't matter. A good time was had by all, and Sister Laughs A Lot Mermaid made sure no little or big mermaids were hurt in the making of the feast.

Meanings: Question your perceptions. Maybe the joke isn't on you. Maybe things are just funny. Everything is not always what it appears to be, for good or ill. And if you meet a colorfully dressed person in the woods with feathers sticking out every which way, it could be a wild turkey coming your way.

Dry Summer
Sister Laughs A Lot Mermaid
***Wisdom:* Look for joy even in tough times.**

Even in the Dry Summer, even in the heat, even in the drought, the Sonoran Desert can be beautiful, highlighting greens and yellows in the sweet light of dawn and dusk. Even during difficult times, Sister Laughs A Lot Mermaid finds joy. She doesn't pretend all is well. She is able to see the sweet light of life even when it feels like harsh afternoon sun is melting the color and joy out of everything.

Meanings: Know that even the worst of times pass because time always rolls on. Find joy, if you can, no matter what, while still being true to reality.

Monsoon
Sister Laughs A Lot Mermaid
***Wisdom:* Enjoy the good times.**

The best time of the year in the Sonoran Desert is when it rains. It can be a dangerous time because monsoon winds and rains can bring damage and flooding. But mostly, the rain is such a relief. Joy abounds! When Sister Laughs A Lot Mermaid witnesses a dawn like this one, she dances for joy, she laughs for joy, she sings for joy, and she calls out to the other Old Mermaids to enjoy it with her.

Meanings: Relief has come or is on its way. It is a time to enjoy the rains, either literal or metaphorical. And if you need to cry—to mix your tears with the rain—let yourself go!

Fall

Sister Laughs A Lot Mermaid

Wisdom: Enjoy the changes—or at least laugh at them.

This is a Gila monster (Heloderma suspectum), the big-bodied lizard of the Sonoran Desert. This particular one was about two feet long. We don't see them often, and it's always a thrill when we do. They are venomous, but they don't come after humans. People usually only get bitten by them when they pick them up. And no one should be picking up a Gila monster.

They got their name from the Gila River where they are apparently abundant (or were). The Gila River begins in New Mexico and winds down and across Arizona.

According to the Arizona-Sonora Desert Museum, the "Tohono O'odham and the Pima believed that Gila monsters possessed a spiritual power" that can cause illness while the "Seri and Yaqui believed in the healing powers of the lizard's hide."

The Gila monster has no natural predators. The only animal that causes them problems are people. So if you see them in the wild, leave them alone. Watch them from afar, and don't ever, ever pick them up.

The Old Mermaids and all the Old Neighbors knew that wild animals were wild animals. If you wanted to eat them, that was one thing. But one did not play with wild animals or stress them by picking them up or getting too close. Wild animals did not exist for their entertainment.

That said, Sister Laughs A Lot Mermaid adored the Gila monsters. She got so excited when she spotted one. She would laugh and clap—from far away—and watch them with delight. Once she got to observe one shedding her skin just before she laid her eggs. How wonderful it would be, Sister Laughs A Lot Mermaid thought, to be able to change all at once like that. Only the lizard wasn't really that changed; she just had new skin. The Old Mermaids had changed when they went from the Old Sea to the New Desert. They had changed their fin-ware to skin-ware. They had shed so much of their old life—unwillingly—for this new life. She wondered if the Gila monster shed her skin on purpose. Or was it just something uncontrollable that happened to her?

Sister Laughs A Lot Mermaid hoped the lizard had some say in her changes. Still, there had to be some joy in stretching and letting a part of you peel away.

Meanings: Ask yourself what about your life can you control and what part is out of your control? Can you come to peace with that which you cannot control? Try to relax into it and find the joy.

Winter
Sister Laughs A Lot Mermaid
Wisdom: Enjoy the joke.

It's winter and time to take it easy. And since this is Sister Laughs A Lot Mermaid's card: It's time to laugh and find the joy.

These two birds are cactus wrens. As far as we could tell, one was the parent and one was the child. The one on the left kept wanting the one on the right to feed it. And the parent fed it. In this case, it was feeding it wax from candles that had melted on this metal candleholder. At first I was worried that the wax was hurting them, and then I decided the bird knew better than I did what it could and couldn't eat. I hoped that was the truth.

These two were part of a group that came onto our patio one day. They were loud. They wandered from place to place, poking around. They went from the dirt to the table to the bird bath to the ground to the table again. And when they saw us, they cocked their heads as if to say, "Who are you?" or better, "Who do you think you are?" I felt like I was watching the bird version of *West Side Story*. "When you're a Jet, you're a Jet all the way . . ." They were the Jets and we were the Sharks. It was all very amusing.

The Old Mermaids were fond of the Cactus Wrens, of course. Sister Laughs A Lot Mermaid had an extra special relationship with them because her raucous laughter echoed their raucous bird calls. Every once in a while, a cactus wren would stop and tell Sister Laughs A Lot Mermaid a joke or she would tell them one. And they would both laugh together, although truth to tell Sister Laughs A Lot Mermaid didn't always get their jokes and the Cactus Wrens didn't always get hers. The point was they had a laugh together.

Meanings: Sometimes you have to make a noise, either to get what you want or to help someone else. Winter in the desert is a time to socialize and tell a few jokes. Find your joy in laughter and making other people laugh.

Sister Ursula Divine Mermaid

Suggestion: **I am most at home where the wild things are.**

Mystery: **Be at home in the world.**

Sister Ursula Divine Mermaid can best be understood by something that happened soon after the Old Sea dried up and the Old Mermaids were left without their watery home, stranded in the desert, drops of the Old Sea beading off of them like sweat. Their bodies were changing, shapeshifting before their very eyes. Before the very eyes of the desert and the creatures come to gather at the old shoreline, some of them adrift, too, stranded in this New World. The Old Mermaids didn't huddle together in fear, however. They drifted up out of the wash, they moved up out of the wash, they strode up out of the wash as soon as they were able. They listened to the whispers of the desert. To the

Earth that stroked their soles, saying, "It'll be, it'll be, it'll be." Then they built their house, their home, their lives.

I don't know for certain but I believe . . . Sister Diana Mermaid who loved the Old Wild Things missed the creatures of the Old Sea. And she missed her Old Self. She was a tough Old Mermaid. Fit in mind and body. Yet while the other Old Mermaids got their land legs, Sister Diana Mermaid still felt watery. Sleepy. That doesn't really work in a desert, you all know that. She didn't tell anyone this, but she felt as if she had lost herself when the Old Sea dried up. Some nights she would try to fall asleep by singing to herself, "My body lies over the ocean, my body lies over the sea, my body lies over the ocean, so bring back my body to me, to me." This was not her true siren song, however, and she still could not sleep.

One morning she watched the sun come up over the mountains, ending one more sleepless night. On this morning she heard the whisper of the mountains. Or maybe it was the whisper of the trees on the mountains. The Old Man and Old Woman talking in their sleep? She wasn't sure. She asked the other Old Mermaids if they could tell what the whisperer was saying. Every one of them told her they couldn't hear a thing. "You know what this means then?" Mother Star Stupendous Mermaid said. Sister Diana Mermaid shook her head. "It means the whisper is meant only for you," Grand Mother Yemaya Mermaid said. "You must follow it to its source."

So Sister Ruby Rosarita Mermaid packed Sister Diana Mermaid a lunch, Sister Bridget Mermaid and Sister Faye Mermaid sang her a blessing, and the others wished her well—and off she went.

We can't be sure of exactly what happened. We've heard rumors. Some say she was up that mountain in a couple of hours. Some say she wandered for days, even months, while she had one exciting encounter after another. Some say she was so sleepy that she was lucky she did not fall into harm's way. My guess is she went up that Old Mountain in her own sweet time, stopping to talk with the Wild Things on her way up. She listened to their problems, offered suggestions, then went on her way again. She probably dropped in on the Old Man and the Old Woman who lived on the mountain. Or they dropped in to see her. And always she heard this whispering. She asked the Wild Things if they heard it. She asked the Old Woman and the Old Man if they heard it. They all said they did not hear it. "It is for you only, Sister Diana Mermaid."

Sister Diana Mermaid continued to wander, looking for the source of the whispering. She realized it was the whispering which had kept her awake these many nights. If she listened carefully, she thought it could almost be the sound the Old Sea made as it stroked the Earth, the sound it made when it came to shore and then went back out again. But it was more than that, and it was less comforting. It was more or less the Old Sea.

Then she found herself under the most beautiful tree she had ever seen. (And I mean she actually found herself there, but I'm getting ahead of myself.) She was up above an old creek-bed when she put our her hand to steady herself—she had not slept now in many many days and she was quite lost—and her hand touched bark. She felt a spark of electricity, although she would not have called it that. She felt a spark. Period. A snippet of lightning. Heat. It went down to her toes. Just for a moment, and then it was gone. This beautiful tree had many branches that were like trunks and the bark had beautiful patterns—mottled, like a snake skin. It looked as though the tree shed its skin again and again to create a beautiful barkscape. Sister Diana Mermaid fell to her knees in admiration.

"You are the most beautiful tree I have ever seen," she said. "May I rest here for a while? I am looking for the source of the whispering that has been keeping me awake. Not awake awake. Just not sleeping." By way of answer, the Old Sycamore let drop a few of its nearly-star shaped leaves into Sister Diana Mermaid's lap. The Old Mermaid rested her back against the tree. "Perhaps I will just rest my eyes for a moment."

Right there and then Sister Diana Mermaid fell asleep. When she opened her eyes, it was dark outside. And the Wild Things sat in a horseshoe around a nonexistent fire waiting for her. She squinted. Wait. There was a tiny flame where the nonexistent fire wasn't. Flickering blue and red above the ground. Across from it, across from her, sat a big black creature.

"Is it you who has been whispering to me?" she asked.

"I do not whisper," the Old Black Being growled. "You have called to us, and we have come."

"But you are not the source of the whispering?"

The Old Black Being that was a Bear said, "We are not."

Sister Diana Mermaid sighed. "I have not told my sister mermaids this, but I miss our old life. I miss my old self. Now I am lost."

"We can help you with that," the Old Black Bear said. "We can tell you where you are."

"Where am I?" she asked.

"You are here," the Old Black Bear said.

Sister Diana Mermaid thought about this, and then she nodded. What the Old Black Bear said made perfect sense. Exquisite beautiful sense. She felt the Old

Sycamore behind her supporting her. She felt the Earth beneath her. She felt the twinkle of the stars above her. She felt the presence of the Old and New Wild Things all around. She felt completely at home with herself, and she felt herself completely at home. She felt, she felt, she felt. Ahhhhh.

And then she heard the whispering again. This time she recognized it. It was the whispering of her own being. It was the whisper of the Old Sea pulsing inside her—pulsing inside every living being.

Sister Diana Mermaid gazed at the tiny flame in the nonexistent fire.

"Does that belong to me?" she asked. She got up and walked to the tiny flame. The Old Bear took the flame onto her paw as she stood. It danced on her palm. She held it up to Sister Diana Mermaid's chest and then pressed it into her heart. It tickled and Sister Diana Mermaid smiled. Felt warm. The warmth spread throughout her whole body. She shook herself until she felt all right again.

The Old and New Wild things cheered. Or roared. Growled. Howled.

"Welcome, Sister Ursula Divine Mermaid," the Old Black Bear said.

And that is how Sister Diana Mermaid became Sister Ursula Divine Mermaid. She Who Is Most At Home Where the Wild Things Live: in her own heart.

They danced until dawn.

She opened her eyes, and it was morning. She wondered for a moment if it had all been a dream, but she knew it didn't matter.

She hugged and thanked the Old Sycamore. She found a stick leaning up against the tree, just her size. When she touched it, she felt the spark again. It flowed through her whole body, constantly—just like the Old Sea. She thanked the Old Sycamore for the walking stick. She looked around and knew right where she was.

She walked down the mountains and returned to the Old Mermaids Sanctuary where the Old Mermaids met her with wet kisses and Old Mermaid hugs.

Whenever you get a Sister Ursula Divine Mermaid card ask yourself how you can be more at home in the world.

Spring
Sister Ursula Divine Mermaid

Wisdom: Be comfortable in the world and be not afraid.

This Cooper's Hawk often hangs around our pool patio and the area of the pine tree. We've seen it nosh on many small birds. When the great horned owl shows up, the hawk does everything it can to annoy the owl until it goes away.

Hawks seem to like the Sanctuary. Whenever I see a hawk, I am reminded of spotting one during a particularly difficult moment in my life. At the same time in my head, I heard the words, "Be not afraid."

Hawks are tough birds. Depending upon the hawk, they are often aggressive, territorial, and skittish around people (unless they are eating). Cooper's Hawks used to be called chickenhawks or quailhawks because their main meals are other birds. Hawks are beautiful, and they are great hunters. You only have to look at this hawk's beak to know that it is an efficient bird of prey.

When they come to our birdbaths for a drink or a bath, I feel honored. They look me straight in the eyes, and I look them straight in the eyes. In those moments, I am completely at home in the world, unafraid and grounded, with no desires, no needs. I am the wild, and the wild is looking back at me.

The Old Mermaids had a similar relationship with hawks. They recognized that nothing about hawks was tame. And the Old Ems were good with that.

Meanings: It's spring time, and a time to go a little wild. Make certain your wildness isn't ever cruelty in disguise. Don't pick on those smaller than you, literally or metaphorically. Whatever is going on, don't be afraid. It will be OK.

Dry Summer
Sister Ursula Divine Mermaid

Wisdom: **Sometimes being at home means listening to the trickster.**

This is a member of the Red Coyote Clan that make their home in our part of the Sonoran Desert. They run in small packs and sometimes alone. They seem a bit ruddier than the average coyote, so that's where they got their name. And they are gorgeous. This one looked me straight in the eye, probably just as curious about me as I was about it.

Coyotes are particularly iconic denizens of the American West. When we first moved from the Midwest out to the Pacific Northwest, we would see coyote skins hanging from fences, as a warning, we were told, to other coyotes. It was as if the ranchers and farmers recognized that coyotes were more than just canines. Of course, every time a chicken disappeared or a cow was found dying, coyotes were blamed. Either coyotes or aliens.

In the folklore of many indigenous Americans, Coyote is a trickster, often tricking itself more than anyone else. On the Sanctuary, Coyote is part of the wildlife. We are often amused by them. When a bobcat (or other feline) is here, we hardly ever notice. And we probably hardly ever notice when a coyote is here either, but sometimes they will race through the Sanctuary, often running in front of my window and then down into the wash. Or we will hear them yipping from many places nearby. In the morning, we often see prints of coyotes, and it seems to be clear they were horsing around, so to speak.

And whenever we see scat around the Sanctuary, we can tell if it's from a coyote. It's always right in the middle of the path, and there seems to be a twist on it, or a degree of expression that is difficult to describe. It's as if Coyote is saying, "Here I am. Shit and all. Deal with it."

The Old Mermaids adored the coyotes as much as any of the wildlife that made their home on the Sanctuary. Sister Ursula Divine Mermaid spent more of her time with coyotes than the other sisters, probably because often she wandered the desert alone, and coyote pups were curious about her. In fact, one day, they steered her to Coyote Mother who lived in a den that looked down on most of the Old Neighbors and the Old Mermaids Sanctuary. Coyote Mother called it a den, but it reminded Sister Ursula Divine Mermaid of some of the palaces in the Old Sea if she looked at it one way. If she looked at it another way, it looked like a shack in the desert.

Coyote Woman stood outside the Den with her hands on her hips with her long tongue hanging out like it was just too damn hot to keep it in. When Sister Ursula Divine Mermaid blinked, the coyote's tongue was gone and the woman was smiling, her yellow-green eyes lit up by the sun. Many small coyote children ran around her and the various cactuses around the Den, yipping, shouting, whimpering, throwing up dust.

"Hey, don't let your brother do that to you!" Coyote Woman said. "Beat the crap out of him next time. Yes, like that. Good. I'll give you something to whimper about if you bite your sister again. You, too much dust, you'll be sneezing all night."

Coyote Woman looked over at Sister Ursula Divine Mermaid. "It's a wild life, ain't it?"

"I suppose."

"The kiddos say you are very serious as you walk around in the desert," Coyote Woman said. "In the summer. They think you might be loco. And not in the good way. Whatcha need? A good story? A run through the desert?"

"A run through the desert sounds good," Sister Ursula Divine Mermaid said.

"You are loco!" Coyote Woman said. "That sun could fry the scales off you in two seconds flat."

"I don't have scales," Sister Ursula Divine Mermaid said. "Any more."

Coyote Woman laughed. "Sure you do. Just like I have claws."

"Sometimes it is too dry and too hot here and I wish it were different."

"If wishes were rabbits, I'd be a lot fatter," Coyote Woman said. "This won't last forever. So come on in and tell me some tall tales."

Meanings: Even if you're at home in the wild and present to what's happening, sometimes it's too hot and dry and goes on for too long, whatever it is. Do what you can to get through it. Like sitting in the shade and telling stories or listening to some.

Monsoon
Sister Ursula Divine Mermaid

Wisdom: Be at home with perspective.

The rains have fallen or are falling. The tough times are over, at least for now. You are above it all. You can look down and see the beauty of the landscape and enjoy the clouds. Perhaps you can even contemplate the meaning of it all. With a wild smile.

Meanings: Whatever is going on, get some perspective, figuratively and metaphorically. It is going to be all right.

Fall

Sister Ursula Divine Mermaid

Wisdom: Be at home with trees.

These amazing trees and that blue blue sky are in New Mexico. In the fall, they put on the most beautiful show. The Old Mermaids adore trees. Most desert people have a special affinity for water and trees. Trees and water provide respite from the seemingly unremitting sun.

Fall is a relaxing time in the Old Mermaids Sanctuary. It's a time to socialize. And trees are great companions. They are never jealous. They never ask probing questions. They never try to shame or guilt you. They never think you are less than or too full of yourself. They are magnificent grounded beings who ask little yet provide so much. In the fall, many of them put on a gorgeous color show before winter sets in.

The trees need us. They need us to learn from them, to be grounded, and to protect them and the rest of the wild ones.

Meanings: Socialize with wild things. Most of the time we need to keep a distance between us and the wild. This isn't the case with trees. We can touch and hug them without harming them, in most cases. Commune with a tree and see what you learn about yourself and the world.

Winter
Sister Ursula Divine Mermaid
Wisdom: Be at home on the Mystic Trail.

Candles surround this stone fountain. The water (which we can't see) is contained by stone—the element of earth—and is protected by the fire of the candles. All of it is surrounded by air. Thus the ingredients for elemental magic are here.

Winter in the desert is a good time to rest, relax, and recreate, but it can also be the perfect opportunity to dip our toes in mysticism. This particular stone fountain is in the lobby of the St. Francis Hotel in Santa Fe, NM. St. Francis of Assisi is the patron saint of Santa Fe. It is said that he was a mystic who cherished animals and protected the environment. He and Sister Ursula Divine Mermaid would have been great friends if they had ever met. Maybe they did. Who knows? A mystic is essentially one who has been initiated into the mysteries, someone who has surrendered to the divine, whatever that may be. With the Old Mermaids, mysticism is an acknowledgment of the beauty and wisdom of Nature.

Meanings: Contemplate the mysteries: whatever mysteries you choose. It is acceptable to rest and relax. Recognize the elements in your own being. What magic do they bring you?

Sister Bridget Mermaid

Suggestion: **Sing, dance, create. If you have to choose one, do all three at once.**

Mystery: **Encourage your creative process.**

Sister Bridget Mermaid hit the ground running when the Old Mermaids washed up onto the New Desert. She knew she needed to learn the songs of their place so she could create chants and spells to help ease their transition to their new lives and this new world.

Every place in the world is enchanted, but if one can't translate those chants or create their own, one will never find the magic. In other words, Sister Bridget Mermaid had to learn the vernacular of the new world to sing effectively in it.

More than any other Old Mermaid, she helped the others re-member who they truly are and helped them find home in the New Desert on the Old Mermaids Sanctuary.

Whenever you get a Sister Bridget Mermaid card, see what it could mean for your creativity. Create, create, create.

Spring
Sister Bridget Mermaid

Wisdom: **Encourage creativity where the heart is.**

Place is sacred to all the Old Mermaids. The Old Mermaids built their home with their hands. They mixed water and earth and their love and longing into a mixture that they shaped into bricks to create their house. They told stories while they worked, and those stories became part of the building.

In this card you see colorful chairs on the porch. In the window a cat looks out. In front of the stucco-colored house are two desert spoons (Dasylirion wheeleri). These are part of the asparagus family and are native to the area. Desert tortoises, pack rats, snakes, lizards, and quail all make the spaces beneath these desert spoons home, at least for a time.

In so many ways, this card represents home.

Sister Bridget Mermaid knew that her sister mermaids were adrift even after they built their house. They had come to this dry, dry land from a world literally awash in water. They came from a feeling realm into a world that often felt windblown and hot with harsh reality every moment. Sister Bridget Mermaid knew that a chant or a song or a poem could help make them feel at home again until they could set down their own true roots. She began creating short magical chants for her sister mermaids, chants to remind them of the beauty of their new situation. Every time Sister Bridget Mermaid sang these enchantments, she felt like she was coming home a little bit more, too.

May the joy of bird songs
bring your heart home.
May the star-studded night
bring your heart home.
May the comfort of love
bring your heart home.

Meanings: Is your home where your heart is? Perhaps you need to remind yourself what you love about your living place. Or maybe you need to consider moving. Most of the time when we change our living places or our relationships, we soon go back to our old patterns and nothing has really changed except now we are dissatisfied with our new place and our new relationships. Make certain you are at home with yourself before you change too much. Home is where your heart is.

Dry Summer
Sister Bridget Mermaid

Wisdom: Encourage your creativity
where Nature calls you.

These are some of the red rocks in Sedona, AZ, one of my favorite places. A prickly pear (opuntia) grows up out of the rock next to a pool of water. Where does that pool come from so high up in the rocks?

So much of life is a mystery. The more we learn, the more we realize how little we know. The dry summer or the foresummer drought is a dry, hot, tough time in the Sonoran Desert. It is a time when many animals and people retreat to the mountains or anywhere they can find that is a little cooler, a little more tolerable.

It's a time to be still. If one is safe, it can also be a time of reflection. A time to wonder how that prickly pear was able to set down roots in rock. Did the rock yield a bit because of the water? Or did the water arrive to help the prickly pear?

The Old Mermaids often went up to the Mountains when it was hot and dry. Sister Bridget Mermaid planned their Blessing Dance and came up with blessings most days and nights that they were on the Mountains. When it was time to head back to the New Desert and the Old Mermaids Sanctuary, Sister Bridget Mermaid helped lighten their spirits with a reminder of what called them home:

The javelina snuffles to call you home.

The bobcat is silent to call you home.

The snake rattles to call you home.

The lizard skitters to call you home.

The cardinal sings to call you home.

The coyote yips to call you home.

Meanings: Ask yourself if it's time for you to do some reflecting. Imagine yourself in a sacred place or go to one, be still, and see what unfolds. What part of Nature is calling to you?

Monsoon
Sister Bridget Mermaid

Wisdom: **Encourage your creativity wherever home is.**

Beneath the desert spoon is a desert tortoise, taking a time out, perhaps, before it continues on its journey. Tortoises are slow-moving, yet they get where they're going. They protect themselves by pulling their head and limbs up into their shell. In a way, they carry their home with them. Sometimes home has to be where you find it. It has to be where you are. Sometimes you just need to pull inside and wait until the danger passes. Then you can come out of your shell and carry on.

> My shell, your shell,
> their shell, our shell.
> My house, your house,
> their house, our house.
> My home, your home,
> their home, our home.

Meanings: It might be time to pull inside yourself a bit. Be still or be creative. Slow down.

Fall

Sister Bridget Mermaid

Wisdom: Encourage your creativity where you build it.

This nest on the ground looks like a work of art. It may be. When the bird or birds put it together was it all by rote or did they feel the creative urge?

Making the place where you live your own can be one of the most creative activities of your life. It can ground you and your family. It can make the difference between living in sorrow or living in beauty. Creating sacred spaces and places in your living quarters can help make it truly a home.

The Old Mermaids built their home soon after they came ashore on the New Desert. They painted the walls with murals. They planted gardens. They told stories. They found ways to shape their home and their lives around nature. They built their nest in the new world.

The sky longs to cradle your home.
The sun burns to cradle your home.
The wind blows to cradle your home.
The rain falls to cradle your home.
The grass yearns to cradle your home.
The dirt lives to cradle your home.

Meanings: Have you made your living space into a home? Decorate. Rearrange. Do you have places in your home where you feel more at peace and more like yourself? If not, transform where you live into your home. Be creative. Emulate nature.

Winter
Sister Bridget Mermaid

Wisdom: **Encourage creativity where your art is.**

This spiral on the Sanctuary is made from lava rocks. It looks different depending upon where the sun is and what the weather is like. The spiral is a common shape in nature. Whenever I see a spiral in nature, I feel as though I am observing the creation of the greatest artist ever: Nature. The spiral also appears in many ancient art and rock carvings all around the world, including on Neolithic stones in Europe, in rock carvings in North America, and in rock art in Australia.

For some, spirals are associated with death and rebirth: We go into the center to face the truth (our death) and come out reborn. It represents the cycle of life.

For the Old Mermaids, all of life is art. Everything they do is an act of art and an act of love. For them the spiral is part of the flow of life, the art of life.

Find solace in your works of art.

Find fire in your works of art.

Find adventure in your works of art.

Find shelter in your works of art.

Find rest in your works of art.

Find wisdom in your works of art.

Meanings: Home is where the art is. Make your life your greatest artwork.

Sister Ruby Rosarita Mermaid

Suggestion: **A good bean is hard to find. Everything else is easy.**

Mystery: **Make magic.**

Sister Ruby Rosarita Mermaid had little trouble adjusting to their new life in the New Desert on the Old Mermaids Sanctuary. She knew she needed to learn a task that would help all of them survive and eventually thrive, so that's what she did. They had to eat. So someone would have to learn to cook, and that's what Sister Ruby Rosarita Mermaid did. It was the best magic she had ever learned.

Other Old Mermaids learned to cook, too, of course. They knew nourishment was necessary for survival. Yet of all the Old Mermaids, Sister Ruby Rosarita Mermaid took to cooking as though it had been her calling her entire life—and maybe it had been; she just didn't know it because she was living another existence in a different environment in a body that was much different from the one she had now.

Whenever you get a Sister Ruby Rosarita Mermaid card, she is encouraging you to nourish yourself and to make magic every day. A cook is the ultimate magician, after all.

Spring
Sister Ruby Rosarita Mermaid
Wisdom: **Nourishment magic.**

On this card is a female Costa's hummingbird, a native hummer to the Sonoran Desert. The hummingbird is a strictly New World bird with nearly 300 species all in the Americas. About a dozen species live in the Sonoran Desert off and on, including the Costa's hummingbird.

Hummingbirds are fiercely territorial. They will fight to protect their breeding and nesting territories. They breed frequently. The male performs elaborate air dances—and dives for the female—catching the light on his sparkling feathers to dazzle the female, apparently, and the female builds the nests, lays the eggs, and tends to the chicks.

They are also pollinators. As you can see on the

hummingbird in this card, pollen is attached to its beak after it fed on nectar.

Hummingbirds have big hearts. Literally. Their hearts are outsized for their bodies, probably because they beat about 500 times a minute at rest and over 1,200 times when they are active. Because they are so active, they need to eat 1.5 to 3 times their body weight a day.

They are also capable of resting to protect themselves, especially during cold weather. Their body metabolism and temperature lowers dramatically. People will find them on branches during this time and think they are dead.

Hummingbirds figure in many American folktales. The Aztecs apparently believed hummingbirds were reincarnated warriors. For the Mayans, the hummingbird was the sun in disguise. The Tohono O'odham tell a story about a time when the Wind left the lands of the Desert People after it felt disrespected. As the Wind went, so went the Rain. Soon the land was in drought. It was the Hummingbird who cleverly tracked down the Wind—by holding up a tiny branch with feathers tied to it to see which way the wind was blowing even a little bit. Hummingbird promised that the People would sing the correct songs if only Wind and Rain would return. And so they did. The Hummingbird is respected for its role in bringing rain back to the desert.

One of the traditional Tohono O'odham songs has a line that can be translated to mean something like, "Hummingbird songs surround me."

On the Old Mermaids Sanctuary, Sister Ruby Rosarita Mermaid was just as fascinated with hummingbirds as all of the Old Ems and the Old Neighbors were, but she knew that some of the hummingbirds were more than they at first appeared. I can't be certain if she ever told this story to anyone else besides the other Old Mermaids—probably, since she was a good storyteller—but it also felt like a secret to her.

One spring day, a storm came up over the Mountains. It was strange because they had heard no rumblings from any of the creatures or the Wind or the Sky. Even Myka Summers didn't mention that her dog Bay had howled or not because that dog bayed every time a storm was near. And one of the Old Neighbors usually had a bit of an asthma attack just before a fierce storm, and she felt fine all the day long.

But the storm broke over the Mountains, dumping monsoon-like rain down the slopes of the mountains that eventually flowed down into the creeks, washes, and river beds. Lightning streaked ahead of the storm and behind it, as though it was leading or herding the storm.

Sister Faye Mermaid watched it and predicted, "This is someone else's magic, not ours. We best go into the house."

And so they all did, except Sister Ruby Rosarita Mermaid who stayed on the edge of the wash a few moments longer. Three things happened all at once: two hummingbirds flew past her, flying low in the wash, but not so fast that Sister Ruby Rosarita Mermaid didn't spot the yellow pollen on their beaks; it began raining in sheets; and water came coursing down the dry arroyo, filling it almost instantly, tossing and turning like a miniature ocean during a fierce storm.

Sister Ruby Rosarita Mermaid was about to turn and run inside—since she was soaked through and through—when she heard splashing in the wash. She looked to her left and saw two tall faeries—as tall as the pine tree next to the house—walking through the running water. They were laughing as their purple and green silk shirts and pants got drenched. They both had green hair, gold skin, and one blue and one brown eye—and something bright yellow powdered their noses.

Sister Ruby Rosarita Mermaid waved. The faeries stopped amidst the tumult of rain and water and wind and faery laughter and looked down at her.

"An Old Em!" the one with the darkest gold skin

said. "I've always wanted to meet one. How do you do?"

"I do fine," she shouted.

"Give her the present," the dark gold skin one said.

The other faery pulled something out of its feather-trimmed pocket, something small and round and golden. The faery bent over and opened its palm. On it sat a yellow cake.

The other faery bent over too. "It's a yellow pollen cake. The bees left the pollen with our mother when she asked them what the druids know. They told her all you need is in Nature."

"Take it," the offering faery said. "May you all know nourishment all the days and nights of your lives."

Sister Ruby Rosarita Mermaid took the cake from the faery's hand. It vibrated on her palm and smelled like she imagined poppies would smell if they decided to have a scent.

"Thank you," Sister Ruby Rosarita Mermaid said.

"Thank you for letting us be ourselves," they sang. "OK?"

The faeries stood up straight. The rain stopped, and the new river began quickly receding. Just like that, the faeries were hummingbirds again, flying away from her.

Sister Ruby Rosarita Mermaid said, "Now I know where birds go in the rain. They turn into faeries."

She hurried into the house, and all the Old Mermaids had many helpings of the Faery Bee Pollen Cake and felt nourished all the days of their lives.

Meanings: Open up to new ways of looking at the same old things. In modern folklore, hummingbirds are often paired with fairies. Fairies almost always represent a kind of eternal youthfulness and energy. Let yourself fill up, just as the dry wash did, with new energy, new possibilities. Nourish yourself. Be yourself. And ask yourself this question: If birds shapeshift into faeries when it rains, what do you need to shapeshift into to let the waters flow?

Dry Summer
Sister Ruby Rosarita Mermaid
Wisdom: **Light magic.**

On this card is the face of a sunflower (Helianthus annuus) against a blue sky. Helianthus annuus comes from the Greek Helios meaning sun and anthus meaning flower. Annuus is annual, since sunflowers are annuals. This giant sunflower is part of the largest plant family in the world with nearly 32,000 species identified and described. The sunflower is native to the Americas and probably started in Peru, although various researchers say northern Mexico, Southwestern U.S., or the Mississippi Valley. It was cherished by the Incas and Aztecs, apparently, and thought of as a warrior plant. Inca priestesses wore gold shields that looked like sunflower heads.

Evidence of the use of sunflowers has been found in archeological digs all over the United States. Sunflowers have been valued by many Native American tribes and used as food, for dyes, medicine, and basketry. It has been cultivated by Native Americans in what is now Arizona and New Mexico for over 5,000 years.

The Hopi use the Hopi Black Sunflower (Tceqa' Qu' Si) to dye wool, cotton, and basketry maroon, purple, and lavender. Traditionally, the Hopi have incorporated various products from the plant to heal spider bites, snake bites, and anxiety.

In the 1500s, the Spanish took samples of sunflowers from the Americas, and the plant was soon making its way around the world, the way plants do.

Herbalist Matthew Wood calls sunflower bear medicine. He writes in *The Earthwise Herbal: A Complete Guide to New World Medicinal Plants,* "The root is brown and furry and the plant is one of the half dozen or so 'bear medicines' associated with the prairie and western environment. Like other such medicines, sunflower seeds contain oils that build up the adrenals and kidney function." Medicinally it has also been used to heal irritation in the throat and lungs and to help soothe irritated skin.

Writer Scott Cunningham has found all sorts of folk magic uses for sunflowers. In his *Encyclopedia of Magical Herbs*, he writes that women ate sunflower seeds to conceive, and people slept with it under their beds so they would know the truth by morning. If someone wanted to make certain their wish would come true—and it wasn't "too grand" of a wish—they could cut off the head of a sunflower at sunset while making the wish and it would come true by the next sunset.

Lots of other creatures besides humans love sunflowers. Depending upon where you are in the world, birds, butterflies, and all kinds of insects flock to the plants. Deer, rabbits, and rodents also like to feast on sunflowers.

Sunflowers are used for phytoremediation. Phyto is Greek for plant, and remediation is from the Latin remedium which means "restoring balance." In other words, it's a plant remedy. In phytoremediation, plants are used to heal the environment, most often toxic soil but sometimes water.

Sunflowers are hyperaccumulators: They have the ability to draw large amounts of toxins from the environment. Sunflowers were used to clean up radiation at Chernobyl and Fukushima and are now being used all over the United States to clean up toxic land, including soil that is contaminated with lead.

Sunflowers are beautiful, tough warriors for the environment.

For the Old Mermaids, the sunflower always seemed like a friendly face, especially in the dry summer when they would long for the Old Sea or for anywhere that was not so hot and dry. Even during those tough times, the sunflower carried on, tall and colorful and sturdy.

I don't know for certain but I believe . . . near the end of one dry summer, one of the largest sunflowers in the Old Em garden bowed its head to signal it was ready; the fruit of its labor could be harvested. Sister Ruby Rosarita Mermaid and Sister Ursula Divine Mermaid went to the sunflower, thanked it, and then they beheaded it. They whispered thank yous to all the sunflowers ever grown. They broke the head in two and gave one half to Grand Mother Yemaya Mermaid to distribute to the rest of the Old Mermaids. Then they headed up the Mountains to pay their respects to Bear Woman.

On the way up, the two Old Mermaids feasted on some of the seeds. By the time they reached their destination, they were not feeling so hot and dry. In fact, they could almost feel the Old Sea coursing through their veins.

As they walked toward Bear Woman's cave, they saw her sitting outside. She did not look like herself. Usually they could not tell if she was Bear or if she was Woman. Today, she was all woman.

"Bear Woman," Sister Ursula Divine Mermaid said. "What ails thee?"

Bear Woman looked up at them. "Hello, Old Mermaids. It is too much for me, methinks. This summer is too difficult. Too little water. Too much sun. Too many deaths. Nothing nourishes me."

Her eyes were milky blue. Her skin was ashy. She usually vibrated power. Now she just seemed exhausted.

The Old Mermaids quickly began pulling sunflower seeds from the half head they had carried up the mountain. Then Sister Ruby Rosarita Mermaid cracked the black shells of some of them between her teeth and handed Bear Woman the meaty centers. Bear Woman popped the seeds into her mouth.

After a minute or an hour or a day, her eyes began to shine black again. The sisters blinked and Bear Woman was standing before them, sometimes Bear, sometimes Woman, mostly Bear Woman.

"What took you so long?" Bear Woman growled. "I could have turned into a bunny rabbit. Or a quail."

Sister Ursula Divine Mermaid asked, "Would that have been so bad?"

"Yes!" Bear Woman said. "Because I am not a rabbit or a quail." She opened her mouth and roared. Or growled again. Sisters Ruby Rosarita and Ursula Divine Mermaid did the same. Bear Woman laughed. "That is pathetic. You sound like cubs."

"Compared with you, we are," Sister Ursula Divine Mermaid said.

Bear Woman laughed and laughed. "Who taught the Old Mermaids flattery?"

"It is respect," Sister Ruby Rosarita Mermaid said, "not flattery." She gave Bear Woman another handful of sunflower seeds. Then she and Sister Ursula Divine Mermaid ate some seeds, too.

"We're eating the sun," Bear Woman said, "including all the raw darkness within it. Ain't it grand?"

The Old Mermaids agreed that it was indeed grand.

And then Bear Woman sighed, stood up, and stretched until she was as tall as the tallest tree. The Old Ems wondered for a moment if she was going to go all the way to the Moon. But she didn't. She came back to them. "There. I am myself again. Come inside. I saved some berries for you."

So they went into the cave and feasted on sun and berries.

Meanings: In the midst of difficult times, remember to nourish yourself so that you don't forget who you truly are. If you're hot and dry, what will moisten you, figuratively and literally? If you're tired and watery, what will heat you up again? If you're getting this card, perhaps it's a reminder to be yourself or to help yourself be true to yourself. Maybe you need to visit Bear Woman or a sunflower. And remember, the difficult times don't last forever because nothing does. You can be as tough as a sunflower or a bear: Eat the dark center of the sun; it's good for you.

Monsoon
Sister Ruby Rosarita Mermaid
Wisdom: **Magic tools.**

Monsoon is a betwixt and between time in the Sonoran Desert. Like the dry summer, it can turn dangerous easily whether the rains fall or not. What was once a dry wash where all kinds of creatures travelled can now suddenly become a raging river. If the summer rains don't materialize, death and destruction lurks behind every bend in the path. Either way, we are standing on a threshold.

In this card, several mostly wooden spoons and stirrers are in a ceramic container on a window ledge.

The sweet light of dawn or sunset comes through the window.

The ceramic container holds the utensils safely, "containing" their power, until the cook decides to use them. Flowers seem to be peeking out from both sides of the container, but we can barely see them. Are they a promise of what is possible if we take one of the spoons out and use it?

The window is closed, but light shines through. Windows are always threshold places, opened or closed. If closed, the energy is contained inside—or what is outside is kept outside. Opened the magic flows everywhere.

The focus of the card is on the spoons and stirrers. Researchers believe spoons have been around for thousands of years. Our ancestors most likely used horns and other naturally curved instruments as spoons initially.

Spoons have been associated with magic for centuries. In Eastern Europe, it was believed that if a person threw a spoon over their head, they would be released from fear if the spoon fell concave side up. Also, a wooden spoon could be used in ritual to break an evil eye spell. By the 18th century, a silver spoon was a regular baby gift in Western Europe as a way of wishing the child prosperity. In Scandinavia and

Wales, male suitors often gifted a lovespoon to their intended at the beginning of their courtship.

Of course, spoons were and are used in cooking. Cooking is magic of the everyday. The cook takes individual ingredients, puts them together, stirs, usually adds heat, and the ingredients transform and become a meal.

Most often the cook uses a recipe which is essentially a spell, a set of instructions on how to enchant the ingredients to create something new.

This card is all about possibilities. In life, so much is out of our control. You can't choose whether the monsoon rains will come or if the dry summer will continue into autumn. If the rains do fall, will you decide to pick up the spoon, open the window, and make some magic, stir up some good trouble and/or good food? If it doesn't rain, will you pick up the spoon anyway?

Sister Ruby Rosarita Mermaid did not know how to cook when they first came to the New Desert. After a lifetime in the Old Sea, she had no idea what it meant to cook anything. Yet somehow, she figured out cooking was her job and her way to bring magic back into their lives almost as soon as they shook the drops of the Old Sea from their changed bodies and stepped into the desert.

She mostly learned how to cook from the Witch of

Coyote Hill. On Sister Ruby Rosarita Mermaid's first day at Coyote Hill, the Witch handed her a wooden spoon.

"This is made from mesquite," the Witch said. "Mesquite trees are some of the oldest people with the oldest wisdom. They send a tap root deep into the desert, and they can find water almost anywhere. The Mesquites know most of the mysteries of the New Desert. Maybe all of them. Wield this spoon and all of your spoons as a great witch or wizard would wield her staff or wand. It is deep magic. Use it wisely."

The Witch took Sister Ruby Rosarita Mermaid outdoors to a gnarled old tree with tiny green leaves and green pods hanging from the smaller branches.

"Mother," the Witch said, "you who know all. Please imbue your magic into this spoon so that Sister Ruby Rosarita Mermaid's dishes will bring healing and wisdom to all who want it."

The Witch of Coyote Hill nodded to Sister Ruby Rosarita Mermaid who set the spoon on one of the mesquite tree's thicker branches.

"Thank you," Sister Ruby Rosarita Mermaid said. "I would be honored."

"And what will you do in exchange for this blessing?" the Witch asked.

Sister Ruby Rosarita Mermaid didn't know what to say. She closed her eyes and tried to feel the tree's presence. She sensed nothing and only heard her own thoughts whirling around in her head.

"I don't know yet," Sister Ruby Rosarita Mermaid said, "but I will."

The Witch of Coyote Hill nodded.

Sister Ruby Rosarita Mermaid picked up the spoon, and the Witch and Old Mermaid returned to the house. The first dish they created was soup from pinto beans.

"Remember, always talk to the ingredients," the Witch of Coyote Hill said. "It's respectful. Everything in the world is enchanted. It is best to remember that."

"Can I sing to them?" Sister Ruby Rosarita Mermaid asked.

"Even better," the Witch said. "Song makes the enchantment stronger. Now use the spoon to stir in more magic. Call for health or prosperity or safety or all three as you stir clockwise."

When it was time to pour water into the beans, Sister Ruby Rosarita Mermaid picked up her mesquite spoon and put it into the soup and began to sing, "Beans, beans, we're mermaid Queens. Make this stew a healing brew."

The Witch nodded in approval.

"That is what I will do to thank the Mesquite for the spoon and the blessing," Sister Ruby Rosarita Mermaid said. She knew instantly that the Mesquite would like this. "I will sing when I cook, and I will sing the praises of the Old Mesquite."

And so she did. Over time, Sister Ruby Rosarita Mermaid collected more spoons, made of other wood. She used an oak spoon when she wanted to stir in some strength to a dish. If someone needed a special healing, she might use her pine spoon. Or if they all needed a little more magic, then she used the hazel spoon. But the mesquite was her favorite until it broke one day. She threw the pieces into the wash during the monsoon, and the water took them away to unknown parts. The Old Ems heard rumors that each of the pieces were turned into spoons that were given to newborn babies who grew up to be great magicians, witches, sorcerers, cooks, or whatever name you want to give to those who are able to understand the mysteries of the world and transform that which was into that which is.

Meanings: You are at a threshold, at a betwixt and between time. Do you pick up the spoon and make magic? Can you transform that which needs transforming? Some things in life are in our control. Step into the discomfort and cook some magic.

Fall
Sister Ruby Rosarita Mermaid
Wisdom: **Creation magic.**

Ahhh, what a relief. Autumn has arrived. The mornings are cooler. The entire day is cooler. You have survived the dry summer and even the mysticism of the monsoons. Now it is the time to gather in the harvest and enjoy it.

In Sister Ruby Rosarita Mermaid's monsoon card, the instruments of power and transformation are there—the wooden spoons—and the question was "will you pick up the spoon and make magic?" Clearly the answer in this card is, "yes!" You did pick up the spoon and make magic. In this card, we see a pan with Sister Ruby Rosarita Mermaid's Famous Blueberry Omelet in it. In this particular pan, if you look closely, you can see that Sister Ruby Rosarita Mermaid mixed blueberries and blackberries into the egg mixture.

Berries were most likely one of the first foodstuffs of all of our ancestors. Blackberries (or bramble) were considered sacred to the goddess to some of our European ancestors. They were tough resilient plants that could be harvested for months once they began to produce. In some places, human folk didn't eat blackberries and considered the berries to be fairy food.

Blueberries, which are native to North America, were (and are) used by many Indigenous American tribes for medicine, dye, and food. Magically blueberries were considered to be a protective food by some Europeans.

For the Old Mermaids, every part of Nature has meaning and significance, not just to their lives but to the world as a whole. And every dish Sister Ruby Rosarita Mermaid created was meant to heal, soothe, and/or inspire and sometimes to protect or inform or bring sweet dreams or answer deep and abiding questions.

The Famous Blueberry Omelet was meant to protect everyone who ate it from harm and misunderstandings.

Two of the children who lived near the Old Mermaids, Whey and Kay, went out berry hunting one morning. At the end of the day, they came to the Tea Shell each with a bucket full of berries. And they were arguing. Whey said her blackberries were better than Kay's blueberries. They stood in the middle of the Tea Shell saying things like, "Uh-uh. Blueberries are mushy." "Uh-uh. Blueberries are the color of the almost night sky. Blackberries taste like water." "And that's a bad thing?"

Sister Ruby Rosarita Mermaid stood with her hands on her hips listening. Sister Sophia stood next to her, rolling her eyes. Fortunately, no customers were in the Tea Shell at that time.

Whey and Kay never seemed to be able to get along. It was as if they were living in two separate worlds. They weren't quite teenagers yet, but they seemed like old people who had been fighting forever.

Finally Sister Ruby Rosarita Mermaid said, "Have you brought this great harvest to gift to us?"

"No," Whey said. "We want you to use your magic to determine which is the better berry."

Kay nodded.

Ah, so they could agree on something. Sister Ruby Rosarita Mermaid motioned for them to put the buckets on the counter. She went into the kitchen and returned with a pan and eggs. She cracked four eggs into the pan, then broke and stirred them with a fork.

"Now put a handful of berries into the pan," Sister Ruby Rosarita Mermaid said.

The children looked at her and then at each other.

"You first," Whey said.

"No, you," Kay said.

"So that I can look like an idiot if I do it wrong?" Whey asked.

"How can you do it wrong?" Kay said.

"Wouldn't you like to know," Whey said.

"Do it at the same time!" Sister Sophia Mermaid said.

So they reached into their respective buckets, brought out a handful of berries each, and dropped them into the eggs. Sister Ruby Rosarita Mermaid stirred the berries into the mixture with her fork.

Sister Ruby Rosarita Mermaid said, "You mustn't say a word until it's ready or the magic will not work."

The children nodded.

Sister Ruby Rosarita Mermaid put the pan into the oven. Sister Sheila Mermaid pointed to an empty table. The children walked to it and sat across from one another and glared at each other.

A few minutes, hours, or days later, Sister Ruby Rosarita Mermaid took the pan from the oven. The eggs had set nicely. She cut two pieces from the omelet, put them on plates with a fork, and took them to the children.

"Eat silently," Sister Ruby Rosarita Mermaid warned.

The children grumbled, but they ate what was on their plates in silence.

"How is it?" Sister Ruby Rosarita Mermaid asked when the children were almost finished. She and Sister Sophia Mermaid had each eaten a piece, too.

"It's very good," they said almost at the same time.

Sister Ruby Rosarita Mermaid nodded.

"So," Whey asked. "Which berry is better?"

"Which did you think was better?" Sister Ruby Rosarita Mermaid asked.

"I couldn't tell," Kay said. "They were all mixed together."

Sister Ruby Rosarita Mermaid nodded. "That's right. How's that for magic?"

"Wait," Whey said. "That's your answer?"

Sister Ruby Rosarita Mermaid shrugged. "You couldn't tell. I couldn't tell. What does it matter? It's a stupid thing to fight about. Take these berries home to your parents. Show them how to make a Blueberry Omelet."

The children rolled their eyes, but they got up and took their buckets off the counter and left the Tea Shell. The Old Mermaids heard one of them mumble, "They're weird," and the other one said, "Agreed."

Sister Ruby Rosarita Mermaid and Sister Sophia Mermaid laughed.

Sometimes it's as easy as that.

Meanings: Create. It's harvest time. You've chosen to make magic. It's OK to relax and enjoy yourself. You deserve it.

Winter

Sister Ruby Rosarita Mermaid

Wisdom: Magic play.

In this card, two antelope jackrabbits are running in front of prickly pear cactus in the desert.

Antelope jackrabbits are large hares (not rabbits). In the Sonoran desert, they tend to like more open grassy areas where they can kick up their heels and run like mad from predators. They breed all year long and have interesting courtship shenanigans, including males boxing with one another. The baby jacks are born furred with eyes open and are ready to rumble almost from birth. Momma takes care of the baby jacks; Poppa has nothing to do with family life. The leverets are weaned a few weeks after their birth.

In the Sonoran Desert, jackrabbits were a main source of meat for the Tohono O'odham.

Jackrabbits were considered pests by many rural European-Americans. The hares attracted predators that might also prey on livestock. And they ate garden plants and crops (probably because most of their predators had been killed). The farmers got together to have massive jackrabbit "drives" where they would trap thousands of jackrabbits and kill them. In one drive, they killed 20,000 jackrabbits.

In Europe, hares were often considered to be shapeshifters and familiars to the goddess. Hares were sacred in particular to the German goddess Eostre (i.e. think of the Easter bunny). In Nordic folk beliefs, hares were sometimes called trollhares and milkhares. It was believed that milkhares were most often created by witches from scraps they found around their homes. They then enlivened the milkhares and sent them out to steal milk from their neighbor's cows. The trollhares apparently stayed just off the trail and then harassed (or trolled) men setting out to go hunting. In some of the stories, the hare is actually the witch, but more often the hare is a creation of the witch.

I don't know for sure, but I believe . . . all the Old Mermaids loved the jackrabbits as much as they loved the rabbits and all the other creatures of the desert. They had special affection for the jackrabbits, mostly because they couldn't tell half the time whether they were jacks or long-eared women dancing through the desert.

The Old Mermaids had heard the jackrabbits gathered together on Full Moon nights, and they all tried to see if this was so. Sister Laughs A Lot Mermaid's friend Jack would sometimes come through the veil and visit with the Old Ems in her woman-shape, but even she would not tell them if it was true that jackrabbits danced in the moonlight.

"If you come upon us," Jack said, "it is because you have figured out how to see us. Until then, nope."

Sister Ruby Rosarita Mermaid took this as a challenge. She asked all the neighbors what they knew about the Jackrabbit Moonlight Dance, and they had no news to share. Several times she asked Sister Laughs A Lot Mermaid to tell her how she first met Jack. How she heard the tinkling of a bell and then came across a jackrabbit woman leaning against a saguaro. She said her name was Jack, she was cranky as hell, and she wanted to find her bell so she could return to her drove. And Sister Laughs A Lot Mermaid helped her find the bell and return to her people—only after Jack emphasized to Sister Laughs A Lot Mermaid that Jack and the other hares were not new to the desert: the people and the Old Ems were new. The jacks had been around forever.

Sister Ruby Rosarita Mermaid went into the wash on Full Moon night a few times and tried singing to the jacks. They never showed. She tried a speech. "We are all newcomers and you are oldcomers!" She knew right away that wasn't gonna get her anything. She tried bringing shiny rocks with her. Nada.

Grand Mother Yemaya Mermaid said one day,

"Why don't you try something from yourself, using your skills? That might be the key."

As usual, Grand Mother Yemaya Mermaid's suggestion was spot on. Yes! Sister Ruby Rosarita Mermaid should cook them something. Only jackrabbits didn't eat cooked food and one shouldn't feed wild animals people food.

Sister Ruby Rosarita Mermaid watched the jackrabbits at dawn and at dusk to see what they ate. Then she went out and gathered grasses, pieces of fallen cholla, tunas from the prickly pears, and some sticks, dropping them carefully into the quilt Grand Mother Yemaya Mermaid had made for her so long ago. She tied the quilt around the wild goodies and returned to the house. Just in case some of the jackrabbits were human sometimes, she created a creamy carrot cake.

That night, that full moon night, she hitched the quilt over her shoulder and carried the cake in her hands. She went out to the wash, opened up the quilt to display the treats for the jackrabbits, set down the cake, sat on the edge of the quilt, and waited for the light of the full moon.

The light came, but no jackrabbits. Sister Ruby Rosarita Mermaid fell asleep. When she awakened, the light of the full moon was on her face. She smiled and slowly sat up. She blinked. She was surrounded by jackrabbits and a huge pack rat, a squirrel or two, a skunk, and a badger or three, all dressed in flashy suit coats or vests or both and all picking through her treats to find their favorites.

Music seemed to come from all around her.

"Couldn't you have brought some berries or nuts, too?" Crow Being asked. They wore a long black dress with a slit that revealed a feathery leg.

A tall jack with ears that went up to the moon, nearly, reached a furry hand down to her.

"You wanted to see us dance," it said. "We aren't interested in spectators. Would you care to dance?"

"Of course," Sister Ruby Rosarita Mermaid said. And she danced with the jackrabbit with the long legs and gorgeous black eyes just as all the other Old Ems showed up.

"We were afraid you had gotten lost," Sister Bea Wilder Mermaid said as Sister Ruby Rosarita Mermaid continued dancing. Then Sister Bea Wilder Mermaid laughed. "Not really. We heard the music."

Suddenly Jack was there. She grinned. "You discovered the key to seeing us," she said.

"What was the key?" Sister Ruby Rosarita Mermaid asked as the tall jack spun her around.

"Seeing us as we are," Jack said. "Haven't you been paying attention?" With that Jack took Sister

Laughs A Lot Mermaid into her arms, and they danced away to the music.

The Old Mermaids danced a long while under the light of the full moon, satisfied that they had answered the question: Do jackrabbits really dance under the full moon? Apparently they did, along with quite a few other creatures.

Mostly they had fun and didn't think about anything at all. When they finally returned to the Sanctuary and fell into their beds, they dreamed they were dancing in the wash with a drove of jackrabbits.

Meanings: Play! Have fun. The winter is a time of relaxing in the Sonoran desert. The rattlesnakes and lizards sleep, but the rest of the desert takes a break from the heat and has a good time. If you get this card, give yourself a fun break and play.

Sister Sophia Mermaid

Suggestion: **Go with the flow—and watch out for waterfalls.**

Mystery: **Be wise.**

Sister Sophia Mermaid is a wise old soul. She is the embodiment of sophia, i.e. wisdom. Her name means wisdom, specifically divine wisdom. To have wisdom—divine or otherwise—usually requires one to have knowledge and/or experience in a certain area or areas. As it turns out, Sister Sophia Mermaid has a lot of wisdom in a lot of areas. She understands that knowing facts doesn't mean she knows everything. Sometimes one just has to be still and silent for a while and try to figure out which way the wind is blowing.

Whenever you get a Sister Sophia Mermaid card, it is time to use your wisdom—and go with the flow.

Sometimes Sister Sophia Mermaid got a little cranky because she knew a great deal and she understood the world, and she didn't understand why so many people did not know a great deal.

She loved most of the Old Neighbors but one or more of them got on her nerves now and again.

For instance, one morning around the time of the Solstice, Sister Sophia Mermaid made cookies with chocolate chips some faery woman from the south had left the month before when she wandered through looking for her tribe. Sister Sophia Mermaid had been able to show the faery woman—who never gave her name—where the veil between worlds had ripped—like a kind of esoteric hernia—and Faery Woman was able to follow her people back into the rift. In gratitude, Faery Woman had left little pieces of chocolate that tasted like heaven.

So Sister Sophia Mermaid made cookies with this chocolate. She ate one as she piled the rest of them on a Tea Shell plate. They were pretty good chocolate chip cookies, but then, how could they not be: Sister Sophia Mermaid had made them, and they were full of faery chocolate.

Before she could come up with a name for them, Rancher Josephson strode into the Tea Shell. Sister Sophia Mermaid rolled her eyes. She was not in the mood for Rancher Josephson today. He always wanted to argue with her about something, and he never knew anything at all—even though he believed himself to be the smartest person in the world.

Rancher Josephson walked over to the counter where Sister Sophia Mermaid stood. He looked down at the plate full of cookies and asked, "Will eating one of these solve all my problems?"

Sister Sophia Mermaid wanted to say, "Of course not." Instead she answered, "Yes," without even a hint of sarcasm or irony in her voice.

Rancher Josephson put a cookie in his mouth all at once and began to chew. He nodded, said thank you with a full mouth, and left the Tea Shell without another word

"Well, that certainly solved all my problems," Sister Sophia Mermaid said. On the sign for the cookies, she wrote "Solve All Your Problems Cookies." Then she ate another cookie.

Spring
Sister Sophia Mermaid
Wisdom: **Be wise about invisibility.**

The great horned owl is a beloved part of the Old Mermaids Sanctuary. Although the owl is sometimes seen as a bad omen in some cultures, at the Sanctuary, we tend to think of owls as wise, perhaps because they are associated with the venerable Greek goddess of wisdom, Athena.

Long ago, Athena was the owl, but through time, the owl became her companion instead, helping her see the truth. Later Europeans associated the owl with witches and not in a good way. The owl meant different things to different Indigenous American tribes. For some the owl was the soul of a dead beloved. For others, it was bad luck to dream of the owl; for others, dreaming of an owl meant it was your guardian. Apparently the Tlingit thought so highly of the owls that they imitated the owl's voice as they ran into battle.

Owls are fearsome predators and hunters. They can apparently see in the dark. And their hearing is extraordinary. Some studies have shown that the owl can hear a mouse's heartbeat at some distance and then focus in on that while hunting it.

The great horned owl is also a master of invisibility. I have looked straight at an owl (in other circumstances) and not seen it. What a great skill to have. Like the owl, Sister Sophia Mermaid understands the wisdom of being invisible sometimes. You may know a lot about some things, and it is absolutely fabulous to give your wisdom voice. Other times, it is wise to hang out and be invisible: We can learn so much during these times.

Meanings: Do you need to be quiet and invisible for a

time? Or maybe what you need is to be a tree or an owl for a while and be invisible. Know your own strength and worth even in the silence.

Dry Summer
Sister Sophia Mermaid
Wisdom: **Be wise about facts.**

These are ocotillos (Fouquieria splendens). Although these amazing plants look like cacti, they are actually shrubs. For most of the year, they appear to be dead sticks in the ground, sticks with thorns. Come spring, they begin getting leaves and then the ends of them blossom into small bright red flowers. Anyone who has given up on ocotillo in the fall is going to miss a great show come spring and summer.

This is true for people, too. Sometimes we give up on people or ourselves when we (or they) are just trying to find the wisdom of our true selves. And so it was with Victoria.

As you know, many people visited the Old Mermaids Sanctuary. It was a place to be when one needed to rest, to re-create, to feel safe and accepted. It was rare that a person had any problems at the Sanctuary. I don't mean everyone was the same. No, not at all. But every once in a while, someone showed up who had completely lost themselves—lost their bearings. This was true of Victoria Margrave.

When Victoria came to the Old Mermaids Sanctuary, she was what some people may have called a sad sack. At least that was what the The Pepperman said. The Pepperwoman said Victoria Margrave was having a difficult time seeing the other side of things. She seemed to be lacking some of that ordinary wisdom that makes life easier.

The Old Mermaids each spent time with Victoria. Sister Sheila Na Giggles Mermaid showed her how to root herself with the trees. Afterward, Sister Sheila Na Giggles Mermaid could have sworn that not only was Victoria not grounded but the tree seemed a little wobbly, too. (Sister Sophia Mermaid assured her that was not the case.)

Sister Bea Wilder Mermaid took Victoria out into the wilds, across the desert, and up the mountains. She showed her ways to embrace the wild in herself. Victoria went through the motions, but by the time they came off the mountains, Sister Bea Wilder Mermaid could have sworn the whole world seemed less wild. (Grand Mother Yemaya Mermaid assured her that was not the case.)

Sister Laughs A Lot Mermaid tried to laugh a lot with Victoria. But, as you can probably guess, after she spent time with Victoria, Sister Laughs A Lot Mermaid did not feel particularly joyful. She wasn't sure she would ever laugh again. (Mother Star Stupendous Mermaid assured her she would laugh again.)

Nearly all the Old Ems had some time with Victoria. It's difficult to explain what was not working, but it was not. Victoria was uncomfortable all the time, and she seemed angry that none of them could make this discomfort go away.

So the Old Ems looked to Sister Sophia Mermaid. Victoria had seemed afraid of Sister Sophia Mermaid when she first arrived. She cringed at Sister Sophia Mermaid's boisterous stories. Seemed pained when Sister Sophia Mermaid asked her a question, even if it was something simple like "can you pass the pepper?" You know Sister Sophia Mermaid: She stood her ground firmly and fiercely.

Finally Sister Sophia Mermaid took Victoria to the Tea Shell to work with her, Sister Magdelene Mermaid, and Sister Ruby Rosarita Mermaid for a while. Victoria had a lot of questions.

"Coyote Laughter Tea?" she whispered. "Did you have to kill the coyote to get it? That is horrible."

"No, no coyote was harmed in the making of the tea," Sister Sophia Mermaid told her.

"What about the Wisdom of the Palo Verde Tree Whispered to the Night Tea?" she asked. "Wasn't that something private between the Palo Verde tree and the Night?"

Sister Sophia Mermaid shrugged. "Out here, nothing is secret."

"That seems rude," Victoria said. "What right do we have to take another being's secrets?"

Sister Sophia Mermaid looked at her for a bit, and then she said, "Is that an unpleasant way to be in the world, when everything is so literal instead of symbolic or mythical?"

"There's truth and then there's truth," Victoria said. "I am in search of truth."

"I think you're mixing up truth with fact," Sister Sophia Mermaid said. "Yes, there are facts. And most of the time truth includes some facts. But not always. Truth often comes with a story. You need context."

Victoria stared at her blankly. "I want to argue with you, but I'm not quite sure what to say."

Sister Sophia Mermaid laughed. "Now, see, that was truthful. And factual."

Sister Sophia Mermaid took Victoria to the trees out back of the Tea Shell to pick some figs for dinner.

"Shouldn't we save some of these for the birds?" Victoria asked as they began to carefully pluck the figs from the tree.

"The birds don't need our figs," Sister Sophia

Mermaid said. "But we do. We won't pick them all, however, so that we have some for later."

"How do you know they don't need your figs?" she asked.

"Because the birds were here long before we planted this fig tree," she said. "They know where to get food. We have to be a bit more deliberate about it. Thus this garden."

"You always sound so sure of your answers," Victoria said. "To everything. Do you ever have doubts?"

Sister Sophia Mermaid looked at Victoria. Then she took a bite of the fig in her hand.

"Do I ever have doubts? About what?"

"Anything."

"Sure," she said.

"You never sound like you do," she said.

"And?"

"It's intimidating," Victoria said. "You sound like you know everything."

"Why thank you," Sister Sophia Mermaid said. "I do know a lot of things." She smiled. "I don't understand what you're saying, though. Why is anything I say intimidating? None of it is about you."

"Human beings have doubts," Victoria said. "They make room for other people."

"First, I'm not a human being."

"You are now."

Sister Sophia Mermaid paused, and then she said, "OK. What do you mean make room for other people?"

"Well, you're just so out there," Victoria said. "And you're so sure of yourself. So full of yourself. I could never be that way. So I feel less than when I'm around you."

Sister Sophia Mermaid stopped picking figs. "I think we have enough," she said. "Are you saying you wish I was less than myself? Do you wish I was less full of myself? Who would you rather I was full of? If you are intimidated by someone else's personality, that's on you, sister. I would never ask you to be less than yourself; none of the Old Ems would. Why would you want me to be less than?"

"I would like to be less like myself," she said. "I would like to be more sure."

"Whether you are less or more sure isn't on anyone but you. If you don't like the way you are, you are the only one who can change that. Why not be yourself instead of wanting to be like someone else? Why not want to be like yourself?"

"Whoever that is."

Sister Sophia Mermaid said, "You don't see a bird asking 'who am I,' do you? Except maybe the owl. But I'm sure that is a rhetorical question. I doubt the trees wonder who they are. The mountains don't wonder either, at least as far as I can tell."

"Are you saying I should be more like a mountain?"

Sister Sophia Mermaid said, "Ahhh, you would not ask a mountain to be less a mountain, would you? So why would you want anyone to be less themselves just so you could feel more secure about yourself?"

"I never thought about it that way," Victoria said. She smiled. "Right. I don't want a mountain to be less a mountain or a bird to be less of a bird. Why should I want you to be less of a Sister Sophia Mermaid? None of that has anything to do with who I am. Victoria Margrave. Full of my quivering unsure self." She dropped the fig she was holding into the bowl Sister Sophia Mermaid had brought out of the house. "Yes! That's me."

"Sister Goofy Wisdom," Sister Sophia Mermaid said.

Victoria laughed. "Oh, I like that. Sister Goofy Wisdom Victoria Mermaid. Full of myself."

This was how Victoria began becoming full of herself and acquiring some wisdom along the way. With every meal she created, she whispered and sang and chanted her love into each ingredient in the hopes of bringing nourishment and healing to everyone who partook. She took a seemingly ordinary task and recognized how profoundly magical it is. You can do that, too.

Meanings: Wisdom is knowing about the world from many different perspectives. Wisdom is knowing that we don't know everything. Don't be dogmatic or fundamental.

Monsoon
Sister Sophia Mermaid

Wisdom: **Be wise about resting and recreating.**

Ahhh, what bliss to sit here, take a break, and enjoy life. This is a perfect spot on the swing and under the pine, close to the rosemary bush, the watering can full of water, a statue of the goddess Kuan Yin, and various stones. Kuan Yin is She Who Hears the Cries of the World, the Chinese Bodhisattva of compassion. When she attained enlightenment, she chose to stay here on Earth until she could relieve the suffering of all.

She is also a goddess of protection. She has many stories and attributes. In some places in the world, it is believed that if someone says Kuan Yin's name in prayer, they will be protected from all spiritual and physical harm. (In the round deck, Kuan Yin is not visible in the photo, but that's all right: She is part of the Invisibles most of the time anyway. Her influence is still part of the card.)

The rosemary growing in front of the pine tree is considered a protective plant. People put it under their pillows to prevent nightmares or under their bed for protection. It is said if you grow rosemary by your front door, your home will be protected. It can also help you think more clearly.

The pine tree is above it all, even though we can only see the trunk here, protecting what is below. (The rosemary and pine tree are also unseen in the round card, but their influence is still felt.) An adobe wall surrounds everything, keeping all safe and protected.

Sometimes we need a time out from our good deeds or from being busy, busy, busy. We need to restore ourselves by sitting in a swing under a pine tree next to Kuan Yin. Or whatever your equivalent is. There is great wisdom in knowing that things go on without us: We are not the center of the Universe.

Meanings: Take a rest. Recreate. Enjoy yourself. Then ask Kuan Yin or Sister Sophia Mermaid what good work you can do in the world. Now is the time for compassion for yourself—and others. Who else needs your compassion today? Be wise enough to enjoy yourself.

Fall

Sister Sophia Mermaid

***Wisdom:* Be wise like a tree.**

Trees are loved and venerated by most cultures. After all, they give us oxygen, they store carbon, they stabilize the ground beneath and all around them, and they provide shelter for so many living beings.

The huge old cottonwoods in this photo have put roots down along an old riverbed not far from the Sanctuary. They are great companions, these big old trees.

Cottonwoods have been used by the indigenous people of the Americas for medicine and building materials forever. Poultices were made from the leaves and bark. The Akimel O'odham apparently used the twigs for basketry. The Pueblo tribes used the wood to make drums. Traditionally, initiated Hopi men carve Katsina figures from cottonwood roots.

Like the saguaros, cottonwoods are sentinels. The saguaros watch over the desert; the cottonwoods watch over shorelines. They are rooted in earth and often in water, too, so they carry the wisdom and power of both.

If you're lost in the woods or the desert, look for

cottonwoods growing up above everything and then walk toward them. They are riparian trees, so there is a good chance you'll find a creek or river and that will inevitably lead you to people. If not, you can always ask the trees for directions.

Meanings: You may need some wisdom from your tree elders right now. Seek out this wisdom. Perhaps you need to stand along a shoreline and listen deeply.

Winter
Sister Sophia Mermaid

Wisdom: Be wise about walking in circles.

Labyrinths have a rich and convoluted history, and no one actually knows where they started. Often historians will point to the Greek myth of the Minotaur. The King built a labyrinth so that the Minotaur would stay trapped there. But that is what we would call a maze nowadays, not a labyrinth. When I'm speaking about labyrinths, I'm talking about a path that has one way in and one way out. The walker can't get lost because it is unicursal: one path.

Scholars used to think the labyrinth was an invention of a matrifocal society because they thought labyrinth came from the word labrys—double axe—which was the symbol of the Amazons. The labrys is a double axe, and it is associated with female deities. At the time of the writing of this book, we don't know for certain if the word labrys and labyrinth are actually related. For our purposes here, it doesn't matter. Some writers speculate a drawing of a labyrinth appearing at the entrances of some buildings was seen as a way to trap evil spirits. Others maintain that walking a labyrinth is a symbolic pilgrimage to the divine or a trip to the underworld and out again. We really know so little about them.

Mario and I have enjoyed labyrinths for many years. We have drawn them on beaches, we traveled to San Francisco to walk the one at Grace Cathedral, and we have sought them out wherever we go.

One of our favorite labyrinths was outdoors at Museum Hill in Santa Fe. One night we went to Museum Hill after it was all closed up, ducked under the bar that was supposed to keep us out, and walked the labyrinth under the New Mexican night sky. It was glorious until the museum dogs started barking, and we ran back to our illegally parked car as fast as we could go. That particular labyrinth is no longer there.

When we moved to the Old Mermaids Sanctuary, building a Chartres-like labyrinth with stones was one of the first things we did. It was a way of making the place our own. (We even wrote a book about it: *Kim and Mario Build a Labyrinth and So Can You.*)

A year later, we built a Cretan labyrinth next to it.

We think of these "structures" as art. We love watching them change as the Wheel of the Year turns. Of course, *our* labyrinths are now our favorite labyrinths.

It took both of us a long time to realize that nothing cosmic or mystical was going to happen to us each time we walked a labyrinth. In fact, for a while Mario figured he must be doing something wrong because he just felt like he was walking around in circles. Over time, the experience of walking a labyrinth has become meditative, peaceful, and often serene for both of us.

We wrote in *Kim and Mario Build a Labyrinth and So Can You,* "The one way in and one way out feature is the distinguishing characteristic of a modern labyrinth. Unlike a maze, where there may be many paths, a labyrinth does not try to get you to take false turns or go down dead ends. It's a meditative experience rather than a trickster experience."

The Old Mermaids understood this, of course, especially Sister Sophia Mermaid. Her friend Maisie Daisy had three different labyrinths at her place, and the two of them would often walk one or more of them, silently, putting one foot in front of the other, whenever Sister Sophia Mermaid visited. In fact, when the Old Ems first got to the New Desert, they walked the labyrinths as a way to get their land legs, get their bearings, and come to some accommodation with this new world. If this New Desert had art like this, they decided, where you could press your soles and soul against the ground, perhaps it wouldn't be so bad.

Meanings: It's all right to walk in circles every once in a while. Sometimes contemplation is the answer—or a literal walk in a labyrinth.

Sister Magdelene Mermaid

Suggestion: **You ask me to tell you about love? Showing is so much better.**

Mystery: **Love.**

In many ways, Sissy Maggie is the innocent heart of the Old Mermaids Sanctuary. When the Old Mermaids washed up on the shores of the New Desert, she immediately fell in love with everything and everyone. It was all a great new adventure for her. **Whenever you get a Sissy Maggie card, know that the heart of it is all about love.**

When they first arrived in the New Desert, Sissy Maggie cried, just as the other Old Mermaids did. She missed the watery depths of their life in the Old Sea. She ached for the beings they had left behind.

But Sister Magdelene Mermaid did not stay in the past for long. She went about discovering what she could do to help out in this new world. She created art on canvases for a time, but she soon discovered she had a talent with threads and pieces of cloth. They seemed to talk to her the way ingredients spoke to Sister Ruby Rosarita Mermaid or the way the stars seemed to communicate with Mother Star Stupendous Mermaid.

The Witch of Coyote Hill was the one who showed Sister Magdelene Mermaid how to weave and sew. At first it was all mysterious to Sissy Maggie. It seemed the Witch of Coyote Hill spun gold from straw or thread from desert plants. And maybe she did.

The first thing Sissy Maggie made on her own was a Mermaid Purse. She sang every sea chanty she knew and every spell the Witch had taught her to make certain the purse was filled with wonder. When Sister Magdelene Mermaid went from place to place, she often carried her Mermaid Purse—and people could hardly wait to see what she had inside.

One day she stopped at Haruka's house and pulled out purple socks partly woven from threads gotten from the pair Haruka's grandmother made (and the goats mostly ate). Haruka gleefully pulled on the socks, put on her shoes, and then ran around the house, singing, "Grandma, Grandma! I've got my soles back."

That same day, Sister Magdelene Mermaid

dropped off a baby quilt at the Begay's, one Grand Mother Yemaya Mermaid had helped her stuff with spider web batting, great horned owl dreaming, and duck down. They pieced together the quilt from cloth that in the end looked like a baby with two mermaid tails, one for each leg. Aponi and Bodaway thanked Sister Magdelene Mermaid as she wrapped the baby in the soft quilt. And then they ate lunch.

She dropped off scarves at a gathering of women who danced in the desert, most often under the full moon. To see if everyone was satisfied with their scarves, the women went out into the desert and danced for Sissy Maggie Mermaid. From far away, they looked like giant butterflies.

On her trek that day, Sister Magdelene Mermaid stopped many places and pulled out many goodies from her Mermaid Purse. She had great conversations and accepted gifts of meals and hugs. On her way home, she stepped into the dry wash to cross it and came face to face with a young woman. The woman stood in the wash, in the sun, dressed in winter clothes. She looked like she was about to faint.

"Hello," Sissy Maggie said, "why are you dressed that way? It's summer."

"Dogs keep their fur all year round," the young woman said. "Why can't I wear my coat?"

"Of course you can keep your coat on if you like,"

Sister Magdelene Mermaid said. "But you might die. This world is not an easy one. You can't bend it to your will."

"I hate the desert," the woman said. "And I hate summer."

"Why are you here?" Sister Magdelene Mermaid asked.

"Everything I know is gone," she said. "This was the only direction I haven't gone yet."

Sister Magdelene Mermaid nodded. She held out her bottle of water to the young woman. "You need to drink," Sister Magdelene Mermaid said, "and you need to take off that coat."

The woman took the bottle and drank from it. Then she asked, "Who are you?"

"I'm Sister Magdelene Mermaid. I'm heading home. You are welcome to come visit the Old Mermaids Sanctuary. We would love to give you a bed and meals. But you can't come if you're dressed like that."

"Why?"

"Because you'll die," Sister Magdelene Mermaid said.

"How can you live in this place?"

Sister Magdelene Mermaid shrugged. "We didn't have a choice," she said, "and now I love so much of it."

"I could never get used to it," the young woman

said. She took off her coat and let it drop onto the sand. Beneath it she wore a long wool dress.

Sister Magdelene Mermaid gasped. "How have you survived so long?"

"I wouldn't give in!" the woman said. "I will decide how I want to live! Nature can't tell me what to do."

Sister Magdelene Mermaid laughed. "I suppose not," she said. "When we first got here, we had a very difficult time, too. But we couldn't go back. Can you?"

The woman shook her head.

"So maybe you could learn to love this place," Sister Magdelene Mermaid said.

"You are telling me I must accept the unacceptable," the woman said. "You are asking me to love what I hate."

"Maybe in time you won't hate it," Sister Magdelene Mermaid said, "if you give it half a chance."

The young woman made a noise.

Sister Magdelene Mermaid reached into her Mermaid Purse, but it was empty after her long day of wandering. So Sister Magdelene Mermaid lifted the hem of her little yellow loose-fitting dress and pulled it over her head. She held it out to the young woman. The woman blinked, and then she peeled off her very heavy dress and held it out to Sister Magdelene Mermaid who laughed again and shook her head. The woman dropped the dress onto the sand and took the yellow dress and put it on over her underwear.

Meanwhile, Sister Magdelene Mermaid stood on the sand pretty well bare-naked except for her shoes and purple socks that matched Haruka's. She held out her arms and stretched. She loved the feel of the air on her skin. She loved the feel of the sun on her skin. She loved the feel of the world on her skin. She smiled at the young woman.

"You've given up all you have for me," the young woman said.

"I've given you a little yellow dress," Sister Magdelene Mermaid said. "That's all. Let's go this way. I know some women who are dancing on rocks. They have scarves that look like butterflies. I wouldn't mind wearing a butterfly scarf, along with the sunlight."

The young woman smiled for the first time. "This does feel better. And you are so beautiful."

"See," Sister Magdelene Mermaid said, "you've fallen in love already."

Spring
Sister Magdelene Mermaid
Wisdom: **Love acts.**

The phainopepla—whose name in Greek means

"shining robe"—is a gorgeous silky flycatcher with a striking crest that makes it look like a small black (male) or gray (female/immature) cardinal. They eat the berries of the desert mistletoe as well as other berries and flying insects. Biologically, they are outfitted for mistletoe: Their gizzard strips off the skin of mistletoe berries so that the berries are more digestible. They are the only known bird to do this.

They are amazing mimics, pretending to be red-tailed hawks, kestrels, quail, and other birds when it suits their purpose—whatever that purpose is.

Researchers believe phainopeplas are monogamous. Single males conduct elaborate courtship flights with other single males. One of their courtship rituals is shown in this card: a male is feeding his intended. The males and females tend to the chicks, so it's possible this male is feeding a youngster, but it looks like a full grown female to me. This looks like a sweet act of love, although, of course, I can't know for certain.

Everything Sissy Maggie does is an act of love. She painted, she made clothes for the Old Mermaids, and she helped out Sister Ruby Rosarita Mermaid and Sister Sophia Mermaid at the Tea Shell. All the Old Neighbors especially enjoyed the Tea Shell when Sissy Maggie was there because everyone felt genuinely loved by her, loved by her exactly as they were. What a nice feeling that was. And Sissy Maggie loved helping make food and bringing food to the visitors at the Tea Shell. Someone had once told her that the word nourish meant to care for and cherish, and that's what she believed she did at the Tea Shell—and everywhere else in her life: She cherished and cared for.

And whatever Sissy Maggie brought to the table—even if you had ordered something completely different—you ate. That was just the way it was. People felt honored and glad no matter what she put in front of them. Not in a treacly way. It was just fun and special. So everyone ate what she brought.

Until one day Fain came into the Tea Shell. As soon as Fain walked over the threshold to the café, everyone knew something fey this way walked. Of course, the Old Neighbors felt the same way about the Old Mermaids, although it was a bit different. It was like the feeling one gets eating chocolate cake with chocolate frosting vs vanilla cake with chocolate frosting. They are both divine, just in different ways.

Fain stood perfectly still in the doorway. They were thin and almost translucent, the way someone is who isn't here or there. Their eyes were the color of blue ice or crow feathers, depending upon where one was standing or looking or feeling.

Sister Sophia Mermaid said, "They are not quite here and not quite there. They are not full of themselves at all. We remember that feeling."

Sister Sophia Mermaid and Sissy Maggie introduced themselves to the faery, and they told them their name: Fain. "I think," they said. "I think that is my name."

"You need nourishment," Sister Sophia Mermaid said as they led them to a table.

"I can't," Fain said. "If I eat food from Another World, I will never be able to go back to Summerland."

"This isn't Another World," Sissy Maggie said. "This is the Old Mermaids Sanctuary, and we serve love. From time to time, everyone needs some lovin' from the oven. That is the nourishment you need to get back on track. Then you can go home. Or find home."

Fain just stared at them.

"Sissy Maggie thinks love will fix everything," Sister Sophia Mermaid said. "Just so you know. And truth to tell, she is probably right in this case."

"As of late, I have felt pummeled," Fain said. "And then I got lost. Or something. It's all fuzzy. I came here because I heard you could help."

The two Old Mermaids returned to the kitchen. Sissy Maggie immediately made a cup of Butterfly Kisses Tea and brought it out to Fain.

"Butterflies kiss?" Fain asked just before they took a sip of the tea.

"Have you ever seen a butterfly land on a flower?

Almost immediately they kiss the flower. It's only polite."

Then Sister Sophia Mermaid brought out a steaming bowl of Sister Ruby Rosarita Mermaid's Healing Noodle Soup.

"Nothing like this anywhere," Sister Sophia Mermaid said. "Full of vim and vigor and hope."

"And love," Sissy Maggie said.

"And love."

Fain hesitated, but then they picked up the bowl, brought it up to their mouth, and began drinking the soup. Sissy Maggie looked at Sister Sophia Mermaid, and they both laughed. When Fain had finished the soup, they were no longer translucent.

Later that day, Sister Ruby Rosarita Mermaid made a feast for Fain and all the Old Ems. It was something to see and to eat. At the end of the evening, Fain appeared to be all there there. They asked Sissy Maggie, "Tomorrow will you show me the butterflies kissing the flowers?"

"Absolutely.

"You were right," Fain said. "Sometimes we all need a little lovin'."

Sissy Maggie grinned. "From the oven."

"From the oven."

When Fain was ready and completely full of their

self again, they went home, and all was well in their world.

Meanings: Maybe you need some lovin' from the oven. Nourish yourself. Or nourish someone else. Love is most effective as a verb, an act, not just a word or a feeling. New beginnings all around, started with love.

Dry Summer
Sister Magdelene Mermaid
Wisdom: **Love light.**

This flowering red barrel cactus is from the genus ferocactus. The word ferocactus comes from the Latin "ferox" which means "fierce" and the Greek "kaktos" which means "thistle." These cacti are stunningly beautiful with red thorns that shimmer in the sunshine, especially at dawn and dusk.

On the Old Mermaids Sanctuary, these fierce cacti start blooming in March and bloom off and on through the summer, depending upon the individual cactus. Sometimes when nothing else is blooming, the fierce cactus will suddenly open up to display these bright orange/red flowers that look like mini-torches in the desert, mini-torches that are attractive to many pollinators, including native solitary bees.

Once the flowers die and the fruit is finished—fruit

that are called muppets, by the way—many desert creatures dine on them, including javelinas, squirrels, and birds.

As tough and as beautiful as these plants appear, they can easily fall over and often do, most often because of some kind of stress like either too much or too little water.

Sometimes these bloom in the driest hottest part of the summer. I will steel myself to go out into the sun and intense heat just to stand by them and soak in their beauty and fierceness.

The Old Mermaids were not surprised to find bright beautiful flowers in the desert the way some people are when they first stumble into the dry lands. The Old Ems know flowers bloom everywhere in the Universe, even when we don't see them.

"Look at that nebula right over there," Mother Star Stupendous Mermaid has said more than once as the other Old Ems squinted up at the night sky and saw pinpricks of light. "It's a flower drawing the songs of the Universe to it, just like the cactus flowers draw the birds, bats, and bees to them."

One night they saw a falling star, and Sissy Maggie asked, "Was that star a flower, too?"

"Of course," Mother Star Stupendous Mermaid said. "It blooms as it falls from the sky."

"I didn't know stars could fall," Sister Laughs A Lot Mermaid said.

"Even stars fall," Sister Magdelene Mermaid said.

"Everything falls at one time or another," Mother Star Stupendous Mermaid said.

"They aren't actually stars," Sister Sophia Mermaid said. "Not like our sun. They're pieces of rock that fall to earth and that's when they light up—that's when they bloom."

"That is good information to have," Mother Star Stupendous Mermaid said.

The other Old Ems laughed, and Sister Sophia Mermaid grinned.

The next morning Sister Magdelene Mermaid walked down into the wash to head home after a visit with Annie Who Loves Birds when her right foot slid beneath her—the Old Ems were still not used to their new selves then—and she fell. Her right knee landed on a piece of cholla some animal had no doubt accidentally dragged into the wash on its fur.

Sissy Maggie cried out as she landed on the sandy bottom of the wash with a cholla chunk now sticking out of her knee. She went to pull it out but stopped: It was all thorns. She was just going to get it stuck on her hands if she tried to take it out of her knee.

The desert had never hurt Sissy Maggie like this before. She didn't think she could get up and walk home. But she had to. She didn't know what to do. Things rarely went badly for Sister Magdelene Mermaid. Well, except for her losing her entire world when the Old Sea dried up. Tears popped out of her eyes and rolled down her cheeks from the pain. She licked them when they reached her lips.

"Laugh or weep, we swim in your tears," Grand Mother Yemaya Mermaid had said on more than one occasion.

Yes, she had several puncture wounds on her knee and she was landlocked, but she was still an Old Mermaid, swimming in her own tears.

Just then she spotted a red barrel cactus on its side out of the wash, under an old mesquite tree, its tap root still in the ground. Several bright orange and red flowers seemed to pulse at the top of the fallen cactus, like tiny suns about to explode or toss a solar flare out into the wash. Sissy Maggie smiled as she gazed at the flowers. They were still so bright, so glorious.

Sissy Maggie looked to her left and saw a stick in the beige-colored sand. She reached over and grabbed it. Then she carefully wedged it between the cholla chunk and her skin. She pressed it up against the cholla, flinching as the barbs started to come out of her knee, and then it popped off and fell into the dirt again.

Sissy Maggie pushed herself up. She glanced at the fierce flowers on the fallen cactus as she dusted herself off. Just then Sister Sophia Mermaid dropped down into the wash and walked toward her. She glanced at Sissy Maggie's knee. Several drops of blood were balanced on her skin.

"Ouch," Sister Sophia Mermaid said. "What happened?"

"I was a falling star," Sissy Maggie said. "That's all."

Sister Sophia Mermaid laughed. "Well, shine on, sister. Shine on."

Meanings: Shine on. The dry summer is a tough time in the desert. Humidity is a thing of the past. Everything is dry. Skin. Humor. Washes. It's a time to hunker down and endure. Despite that, cacti still bloom. Birds still lay eggs and chicks hatch out. Life endures if the dry summer doesn't go on too long. This card encourages you to shine on, even during tough times. When you fall, pick yourself up again and carry on.

Monsoon
Sister Magdelene Mermaid
Wisdom: **Love rain.**

The Sonoran Desert receives between 3-15 inches of rain a year. That is a very dry desert. Yet even with that little bit of water, the desert can thrive. Climate change is having a drastic and deleterious effect on the flora and fauna of the desert. The increase in temperatures as well as the decrease in rainfall is causing problems in beloved and stalwart species like the saguaro and the desert tortoise. Many tortoises are dying of dehydration and starvation. Those remaining are often predated on by mammals like coyotes who may have switched to tortoises because their preferred prey have disappeared.

Monsoons feel like a miracle every year, a magic time, a threshold time. A time when everyone counts on Nature to save everything, including the saguaros and tortoises.

In the card, a mesquite tree is lit by the sun as the rain falls. Beneath the tree are several golden barrel cacti—sometimes called "golden ball" cacti. These cacti seem to be collecting the light on their thorns.

Mesquite trees are important deciduous trees for the Southwest United States. They are pollinated mostly by bees. Bruchid beetle larvae drill into the mesquite pods and lay their eggs. When the larvae hatch, they feed on the beans inside the pods. Many other animals feast on the pods, too, including humans.

The mesquite tree has the deepest living tree root ever documented at 160 feet. They are very grounded beings. They can survive in the desert without much water for a very long time.

They coevolved with large herbivores. I love imagining these huge old mastodons and ground sloths feasting on mesquite tree pods. I don't know if the ancient mesquites were giants then or just shrubs to the giant critters. As time went on and the climate changed, mesquite took up residence in floodplains and washes, helping to prevent erosion. They formed huge dense forests called bosques. They provided food and shelter for millions of animals. Most of the bosques no longer exist, at least not as they once did, mostly because of human expansion, but mesquite trees remain.

Everyone in and around the Old Mermaids Sanctuary loved the monsoon rains, although they didn't call it that. Some years they named it Needed Rain. But when it came in a welcome torrent with winds and flooding and thunder and lightning, the Old Ems called it Dancing Rain. Everyone was just so happy that it had finally rained that they all went out and danced.

Sister Magdelene Mermaid particularly loved the monsoons. No matter if the accompanying winds caused more than a bit of destruction sometimes. No matter if the monsoon rains sometimes caused flooding. Any time the gray and black clouds began hunkering down by the mountains before moving to the valley, Sissy Maggie would stand outside with her arms open to the sky and say, "Let it rain, let it rain, let it rain!" And then when the Dancing Rains came, Sissy Maggie continued to dance up a storm for as long as she could. She knew every drop of water was more valuable than gold.

Meanings: Let it rain. This is a betwixt and between time. When it rains, we are in a new and different world for a time. Everything changes, especially in the desert. The veils between worlds become thin. We can step through them sometimes and return again with new knowledge. Honor this changing time. Honor the changes in yourself. Allow yourself to slip into another world or another viewpoint or another way of being in the world. Be a mystic, even if only for a short time, and surrender to Nature.

Fall
Sister Magdelene Mermaid
Wisdom: **Love dance.**

This beloved Old Mesquite grows a short distance from a wash that used to be a river—and sometimes still is during the monsoon rains. Beyond it, huge old cottonwoods grow on the shores of the wash. This Old Mesquite may have been part of one of the riparian mesquite bosques—forests—growing in and around Tucson. Most of these forests have been cleared for homes or died out as the water table fell from water being pumped into private and public wells. Even the very deeply-rooted mesquite trees have trouble finding water when there isn't any.

In this photo, the mesquite and the cottonwoods are lush and green. The mesquite will soon lose its tiny leaves, and the cottonwoods will turn a brilliant yellow. For now, they are all in living color.

The mesquite is bent with long branches reaching out across the way, reaching toward the east and the rising sun. This tree could have been bent by human intervention or by nature. It may have been shaped by humans as a trail marker, although this seems unlikely given it is so close to a river which would have been its own marker. It may have been pruned on the west side because of a nearby fence. The wind isn't so strong in that area to bend it, I don't believe. Whatever the reason, it reaches out. It balances itself like a dancer. Every time I visit it, I think of dryads and wonder who is within and what amazing music are they dancing to.

I don't know for certain, but I believe . . . on or near the Old Mermaids Sanctuary one day, Sister Magdelene Mermaid came out of one of the bigger washes, the one they called Nearly Always River even though that was kind of wishful thinking because if was nearly always a dry wash. She came up out of the arroyo in a different spot than was usual for her. As she went up the embankment, she noticed a tall barked woman leaning across the path, reaching out as if to ask Sissy Maggie for a dance. Sissy Maggie blinked. Perhaps it was a tree and not a woman? Didn't matter. Sissy Maggie curtsied and put out her hand. "Of course, I will have this dance with you."

So under the bright blue desert sky, Sissy Maggie and the Mesquite Woman danced with one another. One of them moved very slowly; the other moved a bit faster.

A few minutes, hours, days, or years later, they bowed to one another. Sissy Maggie said, "I see the dryad in you."

She was certain she heard Mesquite Woman say, "And I see the tree in you."

It was a case of the wild seeing the wild.

It was not the last time the two of them danced together.

Meanings: Fall is a time of respite, of relaxation, of socializing if you feel like it. We don't necessarily have to socialize with our own species; we can share a dance with whatever or whoever obliges us.

Winter

Sister Magdelene Mermaid

Wisdom: Love peace and rest.

Ahhh, winter. A time for rest, reflection, and relaxation on the Old Mermaids Sanctuary and everywhere in the Sonoran Desert. Peace seems to surround two empty chairs next to a small table with a small mermaid statue on it in this card. Judging from the light, the sun is low in the sky, and it's near dusk. To the left of the table and chairs is a rickety wooden fence. Yellow petals or yellow leaves litter the ground. Quiet and peace abound. This is a place where one can sit and observe the world or have a conversation with a human friend—or a nearby tree or cottontail.

Meanings: This card is a reminder that you are part of Nature and humankind. Seek or allow peace with stillness or deep conversation.

Grand Mother Yemaya Mermaid

Suggestion: **Laugh or weep. We swim in your tears.**

Mystery: **Flow.**

Some time after the Old Sea dried up and the Old Mermaids washed up on the shores of the New Desert, Grand Mother Yemaya Mermaid decided she wanted to find a way to comfort the Old Mermaids who were far from home and lonesome for Old Friends and the Old Sea.

It wasn't that the Old Mermaids weren't happy in the Old Mermaids Sanctuary creating their home and making new acquaintances with the furred, the flying, and the friendly. Still, Grand Mother Yemaya Mermaid had seen the tears and heard the longing in the voices of the Old Mermaids when they spoke of their life before the New Desert. Grand Mother Yemaya Mermaid was the oldest of the Old Mermaids after all, and she wanted to gift the Old Mermaids with something that would bring them comfort all the days and all the nights.

Grand Mother Yemaya Mermaid began wandering the wash and thereabouts looking for those things which would bring the Old Mermaids comfort. Now this you probably already know, but I will say it again: Grand Mother Yemaya Mermaid was the wisest of the wisest of the Old Mermaids. She had known the Old Sea was drying up long before anyone else. She knew the paths of the stars in the Old Sky. She knew the difference between the smell of rain and the smell of snow, even before she had ever seen snow. She knew the languages of the birds and the bees and the winds and the trees. And she could sit with Old Woman and Old Man of the Mountains and discuss the affairs of the mountains, desert, rivers, and forests with clarity, humor, and insight—as though Old Woman, Old Man, and Grand Mother Yemaya Mermaid had been friends since the beginning of time. And perhaps they had been.

So Grand Mother Yemaya Mermaid understood that "things" would not make the Old Mermaids happy. Still, she knew that each place had a way of being, a natural flow, a kind of enchantment about it. And the Old Mermaids needed help finding the flow of this seemingly still and prickly New Desert, they needed help discovering the enchantments of the New Desert, and just maybe a found object from their new world would help with this.

Grand Mother Yemaya Mermaid did find all sorts of objects in the New Desert: rocks, feathers, bones, and wood. She let it all be. While each object was beautiful and profound in its own way and Grand Mother Yemaya Mermaid could have spent forever out in the desert admiring and contemplating each piece, none of them was quite what she needed for the Old Mermaids.

One day, Grand Mother Yemaya Mermaid came upon the home of Louie, the Man Who Collects, and Betty, the Woman Who Weaves. Louie and Betty had been to the Old Mermaids Sanctuary many times. Louie had a standing invitation to sample Sister Ruby Rosarita Mermaid's soups since he was somewhat of a soup connoisseur himself. Louie could smell one of Sister Ruby Rosarita Mermaid's soups before she even started one, so Grand Mother Yemaya Mermaid often saw him in the sanctuary.

This day, Louie, the Man Who Collects, greeted Grand Mother Yemaya Mermaid and asked her in for lunch. Betty, the Woman Who Weaves, was not at home so Louie and Grand Mother Yemaya Mermaid sat together and ate squash soup, mostly in silence, listening to the other sip the deep golden liquid.

When they were finished, Grand Mother Yemaya Mermaid said, "Sometimes it feels as though we are far far from home. But today is not one of those days."

"What brings you to this part of the desert?" the Man Who Collects asked.

"I was looking for something that would comfort the Old Mermaids when they are feeling homesad."

Louie, the Man Who Collects, nodded. "That reminds me of the story of Betty's comforter. She knows the story better than I do, since it happened to her. But she is out today with the other weavers, coaxing string and thread from desert plants. She's spent her whole life in this desert. She grew up not far from here, you know. This desert can be harsh. Her parents were very poor, and one year they had not had rain for a longer while than usual and things were going badly for them. Betty's clothes were threadbare. She didn't even have a blanket to keep her warm on those cold desert nights. This went on for some time.

"Then one night Betty remembers waking up and hearing her mother and father out under the moon, over by an agave plant, singing and rattling and praying. She fell back to sleep the way children do. She couldn't be sure, but she thinks it was the next morning when she awakened feeling warm and comforted. She lay in her bed savoring this wonderful feeling for several minutes before she realized she was covered in a quilt. She pulled it off and looked at it. It looked as though someone had sewn pieces of the desert together with an almost translucent blue thread: leaves, prickly pear pads, bones, feathers. Yet when she touched it, it was cloth—beautiful, soft, warm cloth.

"She ran out to the kitchen where her parents were making breakfast. She thanked them for the quilt. 'You are welcome, daughter,' her mother said, 'but it was Grandmother Spider who answered our prayers. It is her thread that holds the pieces of desert together in your comforter. It would be good if you went out and thanked her.' Betty ran to the agave plant, where she saw a small pale blue green spider weaving a web between the thick succulent agave leaves. And curling off these leaves were strands of thread the same color as the plant and the spider. Betty thanked Grandmother Spider. It was that day she decided to become a weaver."

Grand Mother Yemaya Mermaid and Louie sat in silence for a time. Then Grand Mother Yemaya Mermaid said, "You have solved my problem, Louie. I will make thirteen desert comforters for the Old Mermaids. Thank you."

"You are welcome," he said. "I have thread if you would like it. I've collected it from here and there, and Betty has given me some from Grandmother Spider. Betty taught me how to make quilts long ago."

"So you've made them yourself! How grand. Do you have any advice for me?"

"Focus," he said. "That's important. Think of each quilt as a puzzle. And of course, sing to the thread and the desert as you're sewing."

"Of course," she said.

Louie, the Man Who Collects, got up and retrieved a pale blue cloth bag and handed it to Grand Mother Yemaya Mermaid. Inside was a ball of nearly translucent blue thread.

"Come by the Old Mermaids Sanctuary soon," Grand Mother Yemaya Mermaid said. "Sister Ruby Rosarita Mermaid is cooking up some kind of feast."

"I knew it," he said. "I told Betty something was cooking at the sanctuary."

Grand Mother Yemaya Mermaid was excited by the prospect of creating thirteen comforters for the Old Mermaids. It is said—though I can't be sure if it's true—that she began as soon as she left Louie's house by asking the Invisibles of the place if she could please find and pick up pieces of the desert for the quilts. And so she gathered up leaves from the mountains and forests. She found branches there, too, and the bones of many creatures. She gathered feathers and the whispers of dreams on her way down. On the floor of the desert, she found prickly pear pads and the skeletons of cacti. She gathered up the clucking of the quail and the hooting of the owl. She found flat rocks, more feathers, and the songs of coyotes. One day she found seashells in the wash. She kept looking until she had thirteen. Finally she sat under the night sky and caught the dust of falling stars. She scooped up moonlight at the same time.

Grand Mother Yemaya Mermaid spread what she had found all around her. They say these found pieces went on for miles. But Grand Mother Yemaya Mermaid knew where everything was. When it was time, she began singing to the thread and calling on Grandmother Spider for her assistance. Sister Laughs A Lot Mermaid and Sister Lyra Musica Mermaid were watching from a near distance, and they told the others that the thread began glowing then, as though it was made from moonlight. Sister Laughs A Lot Mermaid and Sister Lyra Musica Mermaid loved a good story as much as any Old Mermaid, so it's possible the thread never glowed. It's even possible that Grand Mother Yemaya Mermaid never sang—but I doubt it. I am guessing she sang the entire time she sat on the desert floor stitching those pieces of desert into quilts. This leaf went with that feather and that feather went with the sound of the singing stream and the singing stream went with the bones of the cholla and the bones of the cholla went with the dreams of the Old Mermaids and the dreams of the Old Mermaids went with the star dust and the star dust went with the seashells and the seashells went with the purr of the bobcat. And on and on.

After a while, Grand Mother Yemaya Mermaid stopped singing and began weaving love and healing and nourishment and comfort into the quilts. "May you never know hunger," she said. "May you know great joy. May you be filled up with love. May you dance and laugh. May you know the touch of moonlight on your brow. May you know the love of a good man. May you know the love of a good woman. May you know the love of children. May you know the love of the stars, and the moon, and the sun. May you know the peace of a blue sky. May you have the curiosity of a crow. May you have the happiness of an Old Sea or New Desert full of Old Mermaids."

A day or a week or a month or a lifetime later, Grand Mother Yemaya Mermaid completed the quilts. As she gazed at them covering the desert floor, she wondered—for just a second—how these rough prickly pieces of the desert were ever going to bring comfort to anyone. She thanked Grandmother Spider and all the creatures of the New Desert. She picked up the quilts one by one, and carefully folded them. By the time she was finished, it was night and all the Old Mermaids were asleep. She took the quilts into the house and to each Old Mermaid. Every quilt was made from different pieces of the desert, of course, and Grand Mother Yemaya Mermaid had sewn a little extra into each one.

Grand Mother Yemaya Mermaid laid a quilt over Sister Sheila Na Giggles Mermaid and whispered, "I sewed the strength of an eagle into your quilt."

"And into yours I sewed the beauty of moonlight and sunlight wrapped around one another," she whispered to Sister DeeDee Lightful Mermaid.

As she dropped the comforter over Sister Bea Wilder Mermaid, she said, "Into yours I sewed the magic of the bobcat, the mountain lion, and the lynx."

She whispered to Sister Faye Mermaid, "Into yours I sewed knowledge of peace and desert magic."

"Into yours I sewed a falling star," Grand Mother Yemaya Mermaid whispered to the sleeping Mother Star Stupendous Mermaid, "and the sound of the Old Sea."

To Sister Magdelene Mermaid, she said, "Into yours, I sewed the love of the mountains, desert, and sky."

For Sister Sophia Mermaid, she said, "Into yours I sewed the wisdom of the New Desert."

"Into yours, I sewed the nourishment of the Old Sea," she told Sister Ruby Rosarita Mermaid.

"Into yours, I sewed the poetry of the stars and the

moon," she whispered to a sleeping Sister Bridget Mermaid.

To Sister Ursula Divine Mermaid, she said, "Into yours I sewed all the knowledge of the wild things."

"Into yours," she told Sister Laughs A Lot Mermaid, "I sewed the hugs of a forest full of giants."

And to Sister Lyra Musica Mermaid, she said, "Into yours, I sewed the music of the stars."

It is said that as Grand Mother Yemaya Mermaid draped each quilt over a sleeping Old Mermaid, the quilt changed, softening and shifting until it was more than pieces of the New Desert sewn together; each became the yielding healing cloth Grand Mother Yemaya Mermaid had intended it to be. And from that day forward, the Old Mermaids needed only to wrap themselves in their quilts to feel comfort, to feel more like themselves, to recall the Old Sea without sorrow, to feel wrapped up in sunlight and moonlight and the breath of giants and the mystery of the Invisibles—to know the songs of coyotes and the mystery of desert faeries. It was a great gift Grand Mother Yemaya gave to the Old Mermaids.

About the time Grand Mother Yemaya Mermaid finished giving the comforters to the Old Mermaids, it was dawn. The Old Mermaids began awakening. Each of them gathered the soft beautiful comforters around them and went outside to watch the sun come up and to ooh and ahh over their new quilts. Grand Mother Yemaya Mermaid smoothed her hand down over each quilt, hardly believing what had happened herself. She was just about to unfold the thirteenth quilt and put it over her shoulders when Louie, the Man Who Collects, came hurrying up to them.

"I am sorry to come so early," he said, "but we were out collecting and found something in the wash that we think you should see."

The Old Mermaids followed Louie into the wash. They walked a long while until they saw Betty, the Woman Who Weaves, waiting for them. The sun came up over the ridge just then, spreading golden light across the desert, giving everything a gold and red halo. The Old Mermaids gathered around Betty and looked at what lay at her feet.

They were the bones of an Old Mermaid.

Grand Mother Yemaya Mermaid and Mother Star Stupendous Mermaid thanked Louie and Betty. They nodded and left the Old Mermaids alone.

"I wonder who," Sister Laughs A Lot Mermaid said.

"When?" Sister Magdelene Mermaid asked.

"When the Old Sea dried up," Sister Sophia Mermaid said. "When else?"

"What should we do?" Sister Lyra Musica Mermaid asked.

"Take her back," Sister Faye Mermaid said. "Back to the Old Sea."

"If we could do that," Sister Bea Wilder Mermaid said, "we'd take ourselves back." The Old Mermaids were silent. "Wouldn't we?"

"They say the Big River flows into what's left of the Old Sea," Grand Mother Yemaya Mermaid said. "Let's take her there."

The other Old Mermaids agreed. Grand Mother Yemaya Mermaid unfolded the quilt she had carried under her arm and she laid it on the desert floor. The others carefully picked up the bones of the Old Mermaid and put them on the comforter. Grand Mother Yemaya Mermaid folded the cloth up around the bones. Then she lifted the bundle into her arms. The Old Mermaids began walking. Sister Bridget Mermaid and Sister Faye Mermaid began singing sea chanties, and soon the others joined it. Then they started the encouragements: "You'll be home soon, Sister Mermaid." "Oh, you'll be in the Old Sea in no time." "Say hello to everyone for us." "It'll be a grand time." And then they sang some more.

When they reached the shores of the Big River, it was near night. Grand Mother Yemaya Mermaid stepped forward, a bit away from the other Old Mermaids, and looked down at the rushing water. The Old Mermaids sang softly near her, their desert comforters wrapped tightly around them. Grand Mother Yemaya Mermaid said, "May you be, may you be, may you be," and she slowly began unwrapping the quilt.

I can't be sure of what happened next. I can only tell you what was told to me. But as she unwrapped the thirteenth quilt to drop the bones of the Old Mermaid into the river, the bones slipped away on their own. Only they weren't bones. Some say a salmon twisted out of the quilt and leaped into the water. Some say a faery slid away. Still others say it was the Old Mermaid herself, restored to life. The Old Mermaids didn't know what happened. It was dark. Grand Mother Yemaya Mermaid was so startled, she dropped the quilt. It fell right into the river and disappeared along with the salmon or the faery or the New Old Mermaid.

The Old Mermaids began clapping and cheering and laughing and dancing in the moonlight and river light. Everyone says that you could see their tails flashing like a thousand tiny colored moons. Or gills on a fish. You take your pick.

Sometime later, the Old Mermaids walked home to the Old Mermaids Sanctuary. Once there, each of the Old Mermaids cut off a piece of her quilt. They sewed all the pieces together with the blue thread so that Grand Mother Yemaya Mermaid had her own quilt.

The Old Mermaids kept their quilts close to them for maybe as long as the mountains stood. Some say once the quilts began falling apart from use and wear, the Old Mermaids sewed new comforters from the bits and pieces of the old quilts. Oh, the stories I could tell you about those new old quilts. They say that any piece or strand of thread from those first quilts used in any other quilt carried forward all the healing qualities of the first, only more so, even today.

And what about that thirteenth quilt that fell into the Big River? Some say it went all the way to the ocean. Others say a whale swallowed it and someone named Jonah used it as a blanket. Most people believe the quilt survived. They say if you use a patch of the thirteenth quilt in any other quilt you better be prepared for change. It could turn you into a salmon, a desert faery, or an Old Mermaid. If you find any of it, sew it into a quilt and see what happens. If you dare.

Whenever you get a Grand Mother Yemaya Mermaid card, know that it is all about finding the flow in life. She knows almost everything about everything.

Spring
Grand Mother Yemaya Mermaid
Wisdom: **Flow with your feelings.**

Ah, the noisy Gambel's quails scurry from place to place on the Sanctuary, reminding us of cloistered nuns running away from everyone. Quails are pretty much prey for every predator on the Sanctuary, so it is no wonder that they hurry from place to place. Adult quails seem to be terrific parents, taking turns watching from above while the babies scratch for food in the dirt with the other parent. We have seen broods as large as 12 and as small as one. We've watched momma and papa take the chicks up into a tree to teach them to fly.

Whether they are happy or afraid, the quails seem able to express their feelings out loud.

I don't for certain, but I believe . . . when the Old Mermaids first washed up on the shores of the New Desert, they were bereft. Naturally. Their beloved Old Sea was gone, at least as far as they could see or hear or feel. Everyone and everything they had loved except each other, the Moon, Sun, Stars, and Earth were disappeared to them.

They felt groggy and foggy and not quite like

themselves because, of course, they were no longer quite themselves. They had experienced and survived a terrible trauma. They would never be the same.

That first night—or was it the second?—darkness fell as the Old Mermaids huddled in the wash together, naked as mermaids who have lost their tails to legs would be coming straight from the Old Sea. Grand Mother Yemaya Mermaid worried about her sister mermaids. What could she do to comfort them? She could not tell them all was well because it was not. She could not tell them what steps they would take next because she had no idea. She knew Sisters Bridget and Faye Mermaid were listening to the World to try to hear what the Wind and the Wild had to tell them. She knew Sissy Maggie would try to find something to love here. But right this moment, Grand Mother Yemaya Mermaid could think of nothing to do or not do.

As the night wore on, the darkness deepened.

"All I want to do is cry," Sister Lyra Musica Mermaid said. "But I'm afraid I will never stop."

Grand Mother Yemaya Mermaid said, "Nothing is forever."

Sister Lyra Musica Mermaid began to sob. Soon Sister Bea Wilder Mermaid was hiccuping with sorrow. And then Sister DeeDee Lightful Mermaid cried. The weeping went around to all the Old Ems. As they cried, the jewels they had pressed into the sides of the arroyo when they first washed ashore began to glow in the dark, one after another: gold, emerald green, maroon, silver, white, sun yellow, sky blue. It was a beautiful thing to behold.

The tears of the Old Mermaids streamed down their faces and fell into the dry wash. After a while, the Old Mermaids felt water on their new feet and thought for a moment that the Old Sea had returned. Alas, it was not to be. The wash was filling up with their tears. The Old Mermaids scrambled up out of the wash that was now a creek as the Sun came up. Several of the New Neighbors rushed toward them.

"Oh, what good luck you are," one of the women said as she took off her shawl and put it around one of the Old Mermaids. "This wash has been dry for a lifetime or more."

One by one the neighbors came from all around to see the New Creek and their new neighbors. They brought food and clothes for the Old Mermaids, and they all introduced themselves to each other.

Sister Magdelene Mermaid put on a long yellow sun dress and opened her arms to the day. "Look what the tears have brought us," she said.

"Indeed," Grand Mother Yemaya Mermaid said as she wrapped her hair up in a long purple scarf. She wiped away her last tears. "It is a good day."

And so their life in the New Desert began in earnest.

Meanings: Remember that Grand Mother Yemaya Mermaid knows everything, and she says nothing is forever. Feel your feelings. Acknowledge your gifts.

Dry Summer
Grand Mother Yemaya Mermaid
Wisdom: **Flow with your strength.**

Despite the hot dry summer in the Sonoran Desert, plants still bloom. The saguaro stands tall all year round, and then in the spring and summer it blooms. The flowers usually circle the top, like a kind of halo or very cool hat. Each flower only lasts about a day and then it closes and turns into fruit that the Tohono O'odham call *bahidaj*. Inside it is a deep dark vibrant red.

The Tohono O'odham have a long rich history with the saguaro. According to the National Park Service, "The saguaro is a focal point in the culture of the Tohono O'odham. Their regard for the saguaro is reflected in many of their creation stories. For the traditional Tohono O'odham, the saguaro is not just a plant, it is another form of humanity."

Saguaros are stalwart. If you have studied runes, saguaros are closest to the rune Algiz. They represent courage, fortitude, strength, and protection. When a saguaro dies, what remains is a skeleton that is used by desert critters for housing. Sometimes it seems as though saguaros are all spine. Whenever I need help gathering up my own strength to carry on, I call upon Saguaro.

We have almost two dozen saguaros on our property, and we love them and consider them our neighbors. The Old Ems felt the same way. Grand Mother Yemaya Mermaid knew the saguaros held almost as many secrets of the New Desert as the Great Tortoises, but she didn't pry. Instead, she followed their example to stand upright, be strong, and wave a lot.

Meanings: If you're feeling weak, journey to a saguaro and see what you can learn from it. If you're feeling wobbly and like you can't stay in this world, allow the saguaro to fill you with strength and help you stay here where you belong.

Monsoon
Grand Mother Yemaya Mermaid
Wisdom: **Flow with the storm.**

The storm is here. The veils are thin. The lightning helps open up our minds and shows us where we can travel during these mystic times. Weather witches or weather shamans sometimes use the energy of storms to make magic—or they invoke the storms themselves.

Weather-working is an ancient art, usually passed down through families. When I lived in the Pacific Northwest, I often called on the Weather Spirits to blow away the smoke or keep the rain at bay when I was hiking until I got back to the car—with harm to none. It always seemed to work. Until it didn't. Something changed at one point. I don't know if it was me or the Weather, but it didn't work any more. It felt like something big and awful was happening that I didn't understand.

I don't think this is superstition, by the way, or anti-science. I believe people had a much deeper connection with Nature at one tine than we do now. At one time, I believe humans were able to communicate with and bargain with the World. Now, no one teaches us how so we muddle through, often getting things very wrong.

Grand Mother Yemaya Mermaid did not try to change the weather or convince the Weather Spirits of anything. But she did talk to them and watch them and try to learn from them. And, of course, when it rained, she went outside with all the other Old Mermaids and let herself get drenched. It wasn't like being in the Old Sea again, but it was still pretty darn wonderful.

Meanings: Has the storm come to your life, for good

or ill? Try to luxuriate and learn from it. Or just enjoy it. Or literally try to get it to rain somewhere. Do some research first. Make certain if it rains where you want it to that it won't take rain from somewhere else that needs it. Or try to make certain. Record your results.

Fall

Grand Mother Yemaya Mermaid

Wisdom: **Flow with changes.**

Fall is here. You've learned from spring, you've gotten through dry summer, maybe you even stepped onto the Mystic Trail during the monsoon rains, and now it is fall. Enjoy yourself. Look at these beautiful colors, the amazing sky, the water, the mountains. This card is pure elemental magic. Can you feel it?

Meanings: Connect with the changes of fall. What happened in summer is feeding this beauty. Go with the flow. You understand the mysteries now.

Winter

Grand Mother Yemaya Mermaid

Wisdom: **Flow with your beloveds.**

"When you're a Jet, you're a Jet all the way!" These are javelinas. They are not wild pigs or hogs. They are indigenous to the region. They are tough and familial.

They will rub up against one another, sometimes all in a tight group, in what appears to be a big affectionate hug. Apparently they're rubbing their smell on each other, to keep track of one another. The whole herd is very protective of the babies (who can't be seen in this photo). Not surprisingly, the Old Mermaids love the javelinas and never minded that they ate too many of their plants.

Meanings: Is it time to meet with a group of friends? With family? Who will you protect? Who is your crew? If you don't have one, is it time to find more friends? If not, are you satisfied with your relationships the way they are?

Mother Star Stupendous Mermaid

Suggestion: **All the wisdom of the ages can be distilled into one suggestion: Be.**

Mystery: **Honor the ancestors.**

Mother Star Stupendous Mermaid loved being outside beneath the night sky. For her, nothing was as satisfying as staring up at the stars. She felt as though she was viewing millions of her beloveds—or billions of her Ancestors.

Sister Ursula Divine Mermaid made a wonderful lounge chair for Mother Star Stupendous Mermaid so she wouldn't get a crick in her neck when she was staring up at the stars—and so she was up off the ground, too. When Mother Star Stupendous Mermaid had been in the Old Sea, she had enjoyed finding a pool where she could sit above the surface and watch the sky reflected in the water. But nowadays, she loved being outside looking up, stretched out on the chair Sister Ursula Divine Mermaid had created. Often someone else watched with her, taking advantage of the second lounge chair Sister Ursula Divine Mermaid fashioned.

"What do you see up there?" Sister Sheila Na Giggles Mermaid asked Mother Star Stupendous Mermaid one night.

"For one thing, I see your face," Mother Star Stupendous Mermaid said.

"Where?" she asked.

"Over there, by that bright star," Mother Star Stupendous Mermaid said, pointing.

Sister Sheila Na Giggles Mermaid followed her pointing finger, and then she laughed. "You're pulling my tails."

"I am, indeed," Mother Star Stupendous Mermaid said. "But truly, I feel as though I can see the whole world here. Sitting on this ship we call Home and others call Earth, moving through the White River. We are going places and sitting perfectly still all at the same time. And we all started there, in the stars, and ended up here. Beautiful and impossible."

"Dearest Mother Star Stupendous," Sister Sheila Na Giggles Mermaid said, "I do believe you just summed it all up. Beautiful and impossible."

"Yes," Mother Star Stupendous Mermaid said. "Look. I think I see the Oldest of Old Ems up there, in that bend in the White River. Do you see them? I hope they're having as good of a time as we are."

"That hardly seems possible," Sister Sheila Na Giggles Mermaid said. "But they lighted the way for us, didn't they?"

When you get a Mother Star Stupendous Mermaid wisdom card, she is reminding us to . . . Be.

Spring
Mother Star Stupendous Mermaid
Wisdom: Honor the flowers.

This is the flower of a barrel cactus. The first time I saw these blossoms I was surprised that prickly plants could produce these beauties. I am no longer surprised, but I am in awe. Sometimes these will bloom in the hottest part of the day and year, and I'll put on a wet cloth mask and wrap a cold polyester scarf around my neck and go out into the oven-like heat to take photos. It is an extremely intimate process taking up-close photos of flowers. In the Sonoran Desert, one has to make certain one is looking out for snakes and rats and scorpions and killer bees all the while, too. I am almost always rewarded with such indescribable beauty.

The first spring in the New Desert was a surprise for the Old Mermaids, too, but Mother Star Stupendous Mermaid was on the lookout for flowers. She could find color in the desert as well as she could find stars in the night sky. Mother Star Stupendous Mermaid believed the stars were ancestors to the Old Ems and flowers were stars fallen from the sky, especially cactus flowers. How else could they get stuck on a cactus so precariously? And so she honored flowers with her love and attention, always.

Meanings: It's time you stopped and smelled the flowers or at least stopped and admired the flowers. If flowers are your Ancestors, how can you honor them?

Dry Summer
Mother Star Stupendous Mermaid
Wisdom: **Honor the cycles of Nature.**

Sometimes I think about how my ancestors lived, and I am in awe. What did they have to do to survive in order for me to exist today?

Dry Summer can be a good time to sit still and contemplate the Universe—or the fate of your Ancestors—as long as it doesn't turn into rumination. That isn't good for anyone. Look at the beauty around you or in this card and just love it all.

Dry Summer can be something you must endure or it can be a time of greatness, especially if we consider our ancestors. In most cases, they probably went with the flow of Nature more than many of us do.

For instance here in the Sonoran Desert, Mario and I change our schedules in the summer so that we aren't miserable because of the heat all the time. I swore if I ever lived in the desert again, I would fit into the scheme of things instead of being upset that it was so hot. So we get up very early in the morning in the summer, we hike or do work outside in the Sanctuary, and then usually by mid-morning we're inside again.

Meanings: Do you need to follow the rhythms and cycles of Nature more closely than you are doing now? Change your routines and see what happens.

Monsoon

Mother Star Stupendous Mermaid

Wisdom: **Honor your joyous self.**

Oh, joy, joy, joy! The male Vermillion Flycatcher (Pyrocephalus rubinus) is looking our way, perched on the bones of a long dead saguaro, getting ready to feast on the insects around the pool. Its name in Greek means flame-colored or red-headed.

Vermillion Flycatchers are the charmers of the Sanctuary. Mother Star Stupendous Mermaid wasn't the only one who adored these critters. It's as if they have no idea how gorgeous and compelling they are—

and then suddenly, they look at you and you know that they are fully aware of themselves.

During mating season, the male will puff itself up into a red ball and perform flying acrobatics for his mate—and he will often court her by bringing her an offering of a butterfly or other insect. They are apparently quite territorial.

I don't know for certain, but I have heard they act as companions for Mother Star Stupendous Mermaid, following her during her walks in the wash and performing somersaults in the air to catch bugs as they follow along with her. They never offer advice. They never say anything. They are just there. And Mother Star Stupendous Mermaid loves that.

Meanings: Sometimes you don't need to say anything. You just need to be in the world, putting one foot in front of the other, or turning somersaults in the air. Puff yourself up, show your feathers, and exist. It is a good thing.

Fall

Mother Star Stupendous Mermaid

Wisdom: **Honor the Ancestors.**

Mother Star Stupendous Mermaid gets perspective by looking up at the Night Sky. For her, it is like joining a huge party where you know everyone and you aren't expected to say a word. It is said we are the stuff of stars, so I suppose that makes the stars our relatives. Or our ancestors. After tough times, being in the dark and looking up at the light can be soothing to the soul.

Meanings: We are tiny dots in the Universe. What could we possibly mean or accomplish that would make a difference to anything or anyone? And yet sometimes we do make a difference to those around us, don't we? Often we have to determine the meaning of our life and our actions ourselves. For each star you see, begin to count your blessings.

Winter
Mother Star Stupendous Mermaid
Wisdom: **Honor the birds.**

Here is another red bird associated with Mother Star Stupendous Mermaid. Maybe she especially likes colorful birds because they are like lights in the desert or stars in the night sky.

This is a Pyrrhuloxia or what is commonly called the desert cardinal. The desert cardinal isn't quite as red at the Northern Cardinal (which we also have here), and it is often mistaken for the female northern cardinal. This male pyrrhuloxia is perched on a mesquite tree, singing its song. Mesquite have an incredibly long tap root, so they are very grounding. Is that why this Pyrrhuloxia chose this tree?

Mother Star Stupendous Mermaid enjoys seeing the cardinal in the desert, too, just as she enjoys the vermillion flycatcher, all the dragonflies, and hummingbirds. They all feel like miracles to her. To be able to fly through the air reminds her of the days they swam through oceans

The desert cardinal is chattier than the vermillion flycatcher. Sometimes the Old Ems sit around trying to guess what they are saying to each other. Most of the time Mother Star Stupendous Mermaid does not try to guess. She is grateful to be in the presence of the Old Ems and the cardinal.

Meanings: This card has the energy of a Sonoran winter: Lean back, rest, relax, enjoy! Be aware of all the wild critters that feel like miracles to you. Admire them from afar.

Sister Faye Mermaid

Suggestion: **The rest is ... mystery.**

Mystery: **Accept mystery.**

Sister Faye Mermaid knew just about everything, except those things she didn't know. When she didn't know, she relied on her ability to string words together in such a way that time stopped or time sped up or energy flowed or energy swirled and minds were changed and life was transformed. Or it wasn't. Sometimes magic worked. Sometimes it didn't. Or rather, sometimes the answer was yes and sometimes the answer was no. The Universe is a mysterious place.

When Sister Faye Mermaid first arrived on the shores of the New Desert, she was speechless. I don't mean she didn't talk. She wasn't mute. She had no enchantments to sing, no poems to soothe. She knew she had to listen to this new world before she could find the right words. For a while, she did not understand the world. The Old Ems were accustomed to looking to Sister Faye Mermaid when they needed to change the way things were. Yet now, it seemed none of them could change anything.

Wisely, Sister Faye Mermaid began to observe her beloved Old Mermaids as they adjusted to the new world. She noticed how Sister Sheila Na Giggles Mermaid connected herself in the New Desert through trees. The Old Ems had not had much previous experience with trees, and Sister Faye Mermaid was impressed that Sister Sheila Na Giggles Mermaid figured out the best thing to do for her was to be in this place: be here now.

Sister Faye Mermaid watched as Sister DeeDee Lightful Mermaid struggled at first. She was so accustomed to the milky watery depths. What was she going to do with all the light in the desert? Until she wandered the desert, listened to Coyote Woman, and later found her own light again. She became completely full of herself.

Sister Bea Wilder Mermaid had no idea what to do with herself in the New Desert, but she went out and learned the rhythms of the desert. She completely embraced the wild. Sister Lyra Musica Mermaid conquered her own fears and learned to live her siren song. Although Sister Laughs A Lot Mermaid lost her giggles for a time, she soon began belly laughing as she cultivated joy in the New Desert. And Sister Ursula Divine Mermaid came off the Mountains with a new name—and the ability to be at home in the world.

Sister Bridget Mermaid continued to encourage her own creative process, and Sister Faye Mermaid followed her example as they created songs and enchantments together—even though Sister Faye Mermaid did not feel the magic for a long while.

Sister Ruby Rosarita Mermaid was perhaps the most inspirational of all—even though Sister Faye Mermaid would certainly not rank them. Sister Ruby Rosarita Mermaid learned a new magic: She learned to cook. She transformed ingredients by cutting them up, heating them, cooling them, and/or whispering sweet somethings to them.

Sister Sophia Mermaid never stopped being wise, and she became even wiser, to Sister Faye Mermaid's way of thinking, because she came to understand the New Desert. Likewise, Sister Magdelene Mermaid was always full of love. That never changed.

Grand Mother Yemaya Mermaid was out to sea for a bit when they first arrived in the sandy realms. She soon learned to find her flow in the new world. And Mother Star Stupendous Mermaid continued to stare at the stars, honoring all that had come before them in every step she took.

Sister Faye Mermaid was impressed with her sister Old Mermaids. They had been tossed aside, as it were, tossed ashore in a new world, one they never asked for, one they never longed for, and yet they had all done their best. They had each risen to the occasion, more full of themselves, more knowledgeable, more capable than they had ever been.

As Sister Faye Mermaid walked the desert and contemplated all of this, she realized what was troubling her was that she did not understand what had happened. How had they landed here? Why? She listened to the coyotes and mockingbirds as she wandered. Listened to the whoosh, whoosh, whoosh as a crow flew overhead in the dry air. She stood in the wash where water sometimes ran, the Sometimes River, and she suddenly realized the reason they had landed here no longer mattered. They were here. They could not go back. She accepted the mystery of it all.

With this realization, her feet settled more deeply into the sand. She felt a breeze tickle the top of her head. And words began to fall from the blue sky, from cacti arms, from the beaks of passing birds. Sister Faye Mermaid felt enchantment all around her in the deep pulsing silence.

Whenever you get a Sister Faye Mermaid card, she is encouraging you to realize you don't know

everything. Sometimes we have to accept the mystery.

Spring
Sister Faye Mermaid

Wisdom: Accept knowledge.

To me, corvids have always been magical, especially ravens. I am certain they are trying to tell me something I do not completely understand even if that something is, "Go away, poor human."

Ravens know everything that is going on everywhere. They understand the magic of every pebble, tree, and feather, just like Sister Faye Mermaid used to know all the magical goings-on in the Old Sea. Ravens know the magic of here and of there. They have one foot in this world and the other foot in another world.

I don't know for certain, but I believe . . . one day Sister Faye Mermaid was walking the wash, and she saw ahead of her several figures dressed in blue-black feathers—or maybe they *were* blue-black feathers. They were incredibly large or incredibly small. As they walked, the air moved around them like waves in a lake move when something swims in it.

Sister Faye Mermaid stopped and watched. As she did so, one turned to look at her. The others flew away to the tops of nearby saguaros.

"Good day, Old Mermaid," Old Raven said.

"Good day, Old Raven," she answered.

"If you follow a raven, you should be ready for trouble."

"Trouble or enchantment," Sister Faye Mermaid said.

Old Raven laughed. Its eyes were blacker than its beak. "Same thing. You used to know magic."

"I did," she said. "I could heal and reveal. Now I am just hot and dry. I would welcome your advice."

"It's spring," Old Raven said. "Everything is new again. Step into that creation. Simple as that. Let go of who you were. Let go of what you knew, at least for now. Every year, I learn it all over again, and it's always different."

"Isn't that exhausting?"

Old Raven laughed. "Ack, ack, ack. Death is exhausting."

Sister Faye Mermaid nodded. "I appreciate your magic."

"I appreciate yours, too," Old Raven said. "I can hear it coming."

With that, Old Raven flew away, and Sister Faye Mermaid stepped into creation.

Meanings: If you have a dilemma, let go of what you think you know. Start at the beginning—at creation—and find what's new and true.

Dry Summer
Sister Faye Mermaid
Wisdom: **Accept reality.**

This is a palm tree with a gorgeous Arizona sunset behind it. You know it's hot just by looking at this photo: the intense orange sunset along with the palm tell you that. Beauty can come from these long hot summers or even from stretches of rough times, especially if we can stay grounded in our bodies. Sister Faye Mermaid came up with her best and most effective chants when she was completely in her body, breathing from moment to moment, even when it seemed too hot and dry to breathe.

Meanings: You can ride out the tough times. Find beauty where you can, without ignoring reality. It's all life. Whether times are rough or easy, try to enjoy the sunset: That's what the Old Mermaids would do.

Monsoon
Sister Faye Mermaid
Wisdom: **Accept the opening.**

The rains are here. The veils are thin. Walk through this portal and see where it leads. In this photo, the path is flooded. Do you continue on or do you find another way? Sister Faye Mermaid had to find the magic in herself and the new desert. What would she do here? I think she would find a way through the portal—and then back again. What about you?

Meanings: You have an opportunity to change your life or change your mind or your situation. Find the portal, find the door, find the window—and then walk through it. Be an Earth Mystic.

Fall

Sister Faye Mermaid

Wisdom: Accept true teachers.

Most of us have some experience with deer, either in stories or in real life. They are incredibly adaptable and thrive almost everywhere on Earth except Australia. Nearly every culture has some folklore centered around deer, perhaps because deer were such a reliable food source.

Clarissa Pinkola Estés says that the sacrifice of a deer—especially a doe—was the work of the "ancient Wild Woman bloodline." It was a rite of revivification, she says: The sacrifice of the deer renewed life. It was a way of becoming the deer: the Deer Woman. This is heady stuff.

Nowadays, I don't feel as though we need to sacrifice a deer to delve into the Deer Woman mysteries. We can ask the spirit and soul of the deer what we need to sacrifice—to make sacred—to hear and understand her teachings.

In a canyon in the Santa Rita Mountains near here and the Old Mermaids Sanctuary are elfin-like deer called Coues deer. The Deer Mother wanders with them now and again and wanders with the Old Mermaids now and again.

Deer Mother taught Sister Faye Mermaid the ancient fath fith (Féth fíada), the chant of invisibility. But Deer Mother and all deer can act as shamans, leading novices into the wild. These particular deer—the elfin deer—are clearly shapeshifters. Sometimes they gather together and put the fath fith on themselves, and then they run through the canyon together, daring anyone to follow them into the wilderness away from all they had known.

Sometimes Sister Faye Mermaid follows them. Sometimes, the story goes, she shapeshifts, too, and leads the deer into wild places they have never seen before.

Meanings: Seek out the Deer Mother. She can lead you to wild places. You must first be willing to be invisible.

Winter
Sister Faye Mermaid
Wisdom: **Accept magic and mystery.**

This is the front porch of the Old Mermaids Sanctuary. It is normally colorful and bright and a place for socializing or watching the sun or the moon come up over the mountains. Only very occasionally do we see fog or mist. Mist and fog create thresholds everywhere. For a little while, anything is possible, especially magic and mystery.

I can't be certain, but I believe . . . on one rare foggy night, some time after the Old Mermaids washed ashore in the New Desert, Sister Faye Mermaid could not sleep. She wandered the half-finished house, gliding from room to room, like a ghost, a gentle breeze, or an Old Mermaid swimming in the Old Sea: She was quieter than a cactus mouse. Certainly quieter than the javelinas she smelled and heard snuffling around outside the house. Quieter than the coyotes yipping in the near distance. Maybe not as quiet as the jackrabbit she had seen under the saguaro up the ridge near the Hunter's place earlier in the day. Although maybe it wasn't so much quiet as absolutely still. Sister Faye Mermaid was not still. She was quiet.

She did not wish to disturb any of the sleeping Old Mermaids.

After a time, Sister Faye Mermaid lay on a bench that curved out from a half-finished wall. As the fog cleared, she gazed up at the sky. *Stars, stars, everywhere; all without a care.* She shrugged. It wasn't much of a chant, certainly not a song. She sighed. She would miss being able to look up at the stars like this once the house was finished. Maybe she would talk to the others about putting in star windows. Sky windows. She liked that idea.

She watched the twinkling lights and listened to the sounds of the night desert. The house and the Old Mermaids breathed all around her, along with the trees, cacti, javelinas, coyotes, owls, and stars. She listened for an indication that the Invisibles were near. She watched the stars for some sign. Any kind of sign. She waited for a touch that would tell her the Invisibles were listening, that the Old Mermaids were not alone.

Sister Faye Mermaid got up again and stared into the milky darkness. She knew she and the Old Mermaids were not alone. My word! They were surrounded by the most interesting varieties of life—different from what they had known in the Old Sea, of course. But here Sister Faye Mermaid could not find any indication of Spirit, or the Invisibles, the Faeries.

Perhaps she didn't know their language here—or the songs, the ceremonies. She did not know what she didn't know, but it was something. It was something that she had always known at any other place.

In the Old Sea, Sister Faye Mermaid had understood that the sigh of the East Wind meant cold and sometimes enlightenment was on the way. The West Wind most often brought storms and sometimes a sense of calamity. Or an upset stomach. She knew if an eel in the south canyon was wiggling out of its hole happily that either something good to eat was swimming by or it was time to celebrate. If she couldn't see even a tiny glimmer of an eel's eye because it was so far back into its hole, she knew hard times were coming. (She hadn't seen an eel in an eon before the Old Sea dried up.) She knew by the way the sea fronds brushed up against her if the tide was coming in or out, and she understood all the implications of both. And always, always, she knew the great Old Sea listened to her chants and understood her questions.

Here. Here she didn't know which or what Invisibles she was talking to. If any. Maybe she was talking to Air. Which wasn't bad. Air gave her life. Gave them all life. Yet her conversations felt one-sided. What songs did the New Desert Air want to hear? What did this place want from them?

Sister Faye Mermaid felt closed up and closed off

and generally useless here. All the Old Mermaids had a purpose, they all had concrete skills—except her. Sister Ruby Rosarita Mermaid was the best cook of them all. Sissy Maggie Mermaid made friends and made art. Sister Sheila Na Giggles Mermaid could build or fix just about anything, all while she told a joke or a story. Sister Ursula Divine Mermaid understood the fauna; Sister Bea Wilder Mermaid understand the land. Sister Laughs A Lot Mermaid and Sister Bridget Mermaid knew all the plants. Sister Sophia Mermaid had the wisdom of the ages in her brain and all through her body. They all had something. And before Sister Faye Mermaid had always been able to synthesize their collective wisdom and act as a kind of negotiator and go-between for the Old Mermaids and the genius loci of a place.

A while back, Sister Faye Mermaid had decided she needed to do something physical to get herself back into the shape she had been before. She went up to Annie's house and asked to take a bath in her big old tub. She figured once her body was immersed in water, she'd fill up with herself again and all would be well. She wouldn't let Annie heat up the water—she thought that was just strange—so it came as a shock to her that the water was a shock to her. She ended up sitting in the tub shivering. When she finally got out of the tub, she looked down at her body and was startled to see herself—truly—for the first time since she had left the Old Sea.

She said, "I ain't what I used to be."

Maybe that meant she couldn't do what she had been able to do before. She felt anchored. Trapped. She remembered feeling adrift. Ahhhh. Freedom.

Sister Faye Mermaid had talked to the others about how she felt. Sister Sophia Mermaid said, "Many religious and spiritual traditions suggest a time of solitude or fasting might be in order. Or you might try a hallucinogenic. The desert is full of them."

Mother Star Stupendous Mermaid said, "Perhaps we were meant for the desert all along. Maybe the Old Sea was just a preparation for this."

"Who meant us for this then?" Sister Faye Mermaid asked.

"Maybe we did."

"We aren't who we were," Sister Faye Mermaid said.

"I know," Mother Star Stupendous Mermaid said. "Isn't that grand?"

Now Sister Faye Mermaid wandered into the front room. She gazed at the wall where Sissy Maggie had painted a mountain scene. Even in the darkness, Sister Faye Mermaid could see and feel the presence of the mountain. It was as if she could walk right into it. On the opposite wall was a scene from the Old Sea. She didn't want to get too close to it right now. She was afraid she might hear the ocean, might walk into the painting and never come back.

She turned away from the mountain scene. The night was beginning to gray into dawn. She had spent another night sleepless. And she had learned nothing. No secrets. No genius loci had made themselves known to her. She began walking from room to room again. Grand Mother Yemaya Mermaid snored softly in her room. Next door Mother Star Stupendous lay on her side with her hands together under her face. She looked peaceful, beautiful.

In the next room, Sister DeeDee Lightful Mermaid and Sister Bea Wilder Mermaid curled up around one another. Nearby Sissy Maggie and Sister Laughs A Lot Mermaid had fallen asleep next to one another. Earlier the four of them had been planning Sissy Maggie's next art project. Sissy Maggie had snuggled up to Sister Laughs A Lot Mermaid, just like they used to when they were young, sunning themselves with a group of walruses near the shore. A lock of Sister Laughs A Lot Mermaid's hair had fallen down near her eyes, in a curl that looked like a seahorse's tail. Something about that made Sister Faye Mermaid's breath catch in her throat. Her chest ached. She smiled and kept herself from brushing the hair off of Sister Laughs A Lot Mermaid's face. She suddenly felt adrift. Ahhhh.

It had been a long while since she had realized how beautiful they all were—even though they weren't what they used to be. It had been a long time since she acknowledged how glad she was that she had washed up onto this desert with these Old Mermaids.

Just then Sister Laughs A Lot Mermaid opened her eyes sleepily. "Oh, it's you. I thought I heard you singing."

"I wasn't singing, sweetheart," Sister Faye Mermaid whispered. "I was just breathing."

"Same thing." Sister Laughs A Lot Mermaid closed her eyes and was asleep again.

Sister Faye Mermaid turned and stepped over the wall and walked into the morning desert. A beam of sunlight illuminated a spot under the palo verde tree near the house. Sister Faye Mermaid stared at it. The spot was gold and green and comforting and wild, and she kept still, so still, so she could breathe in the mystery of it all. The desert breathed with her. The spot breathed with her. Then the spot turned its head. Sister Faye Mermaid was looking directly into two eyes filled with sunlight.

She blinked, not understanding what she was seeing. Two tufted ears. This was how the desert faeries looked, according to Annie Who Loves Birds. Sister Faye Mermaid heard herself singing. Had she been singing all along? The spot got up and moved out of the light. Something or someone shifted. The desert faery was really a bobcat—or the other way around—and it was looking directly at her as if to say, "You called me. Now what?" The bobcat slowly walked away. It stopped and looked back at Sister Faye Mermaid. She grinned. She couldn't wait to tell the others. *Later*. She'd let sleeping beauties sleep for now. The bobcat desert faery disappeared; Sister Faye Mermaid followed.

Meanings: Are you missing the magic and mystery in your own life? Have you had some romanticized view of what your life should be? Look around and see the truth of your life, for good or ill. Love what you love. Change what you can of the things you don't love. And follow the mystery sometimes. Or decide to let the mystery be.

Readings and Spreads

Get to know the cards first. See which cards call to you the most. This will probably change over time. The cards are full of details. Think of each card as a dream or an art piece that you can interpret over and over. Their meanings will change for you. For instance if one day you have an experience with a deer, the card with a deer on it will mean something different to you than before you had that experience.

Your own intuition and your own feelings for each card mean more than anything I have written about any of them. The Old Mermaids Wisdom Cards are not predicting the future for you. They are helping you have a full, happy, productive, inspiring life. Go have fun with them!

As I mentioned earlier, my favorite thing to do is choose a card in the morning and ask, "What wisdom do I need today?"

At the end of the day, I often pick another card and ask for some perspective about the day.

Get to Know the Deck

To get to know the deck, I suggest you pull a random card for each day and explore what it means to you. Put that card away so you don't choose it again for 65 days. What did each card mean for you each day? Look at the card and see what it says to you before reading anything about it.

Pick An Old Mermaid A Week

Choose a new Old Mermaid each week and explore her five seasons. See what the cards mean to you before reading anything about them. Take notes.

Pick a Season

Choose one of the five seasons and then explore the cards for that season in any way you wish. Get to know the cards before reading about them.

Explore the Mysteries from The Old Mermaids Mystery School

With or without the book, *The Old Mermaids Mystery School*, use the five cards for each Old Mermaid and explore what they mean for you regarding the mysteries. In this book each Old Mermaid's mystery appears on the first page of the section for that Old Mermaid. For instance, Sister Sheila Na Giggles Mermaid is aligned with the mystery: Be here now. Ask how can she help you "be here now" with her five seasonal cards? Make up your own practice for each card and/or use the practices from the book *The Old Mermaids Mystery School* for each Old Mermaid. Remember, this is all about co-creation: you and the Old Mermaids and the world.

Stepping onto the Mystic Trail via the Labyrinth
Ask the question: How can I step onto the Mystic Trail? You can be a Sanctuary Mystic, Nature Mystic, Earth Mystic, Sky Mystic. It's about a deep connection with the divine, the unknowable, the mysteries.

For this reading (see diagram on page 255) you can choose all seven cards randomly. If you're using the entire deck, just choose one card after you ask the question (which you'll find on the following page) and place each one face down until you are ready to do the reading.

Another way to do this reading is to first separate out all the cards for Sister Sheila Na Giggles Mermaid, Sister Ruby Rosarita Mermaid, Sister DeeDee Lightful Mermaid, Sister Bridget Mermaid, Sister Faye Mermaid, and Sister Magdelene Mermaid. Put the remaining cards aside for now. For the first card for this reading, ask the question, and then choose one of Sister Sheila Na Giggles Mermaid cards and place it face down in the first circle (grounding), and do that all the way around according to which Old Mermaid goes with which circle.

Then turn them over one at a time and complete the reading. For the seventh and final card put all the remaining cards together, shuffle, cut the cards three ways and pick the top card of the first pile of the three cuts, and place it on the circle face down.

1. How can I ground myself for this journey on the Mystic Trail? Choose from the five Sister Sheila Na Giggles Mermaid cards.

2. How can I find/create magic during this journey? Choose from one of the five Sister Ruby Rosarita Mermaid cards.

3. How can I be full of my true self during this journey? Choose from one of the five Sister DeeDee Lightful Mermaid cards.

4. How can I be creative during this journey? Choose a Sister Bridget Mermaid card.

5. How can I connect with the Invisibles during this journey? Choose a Sister Faye Mermaid card.

6. How can I love and be loving during this journey? Choose a Sister Magdelene Mermaid card.

7. At the center: This represents you and who you will become on this journey. Choose from the remainder of the deck.

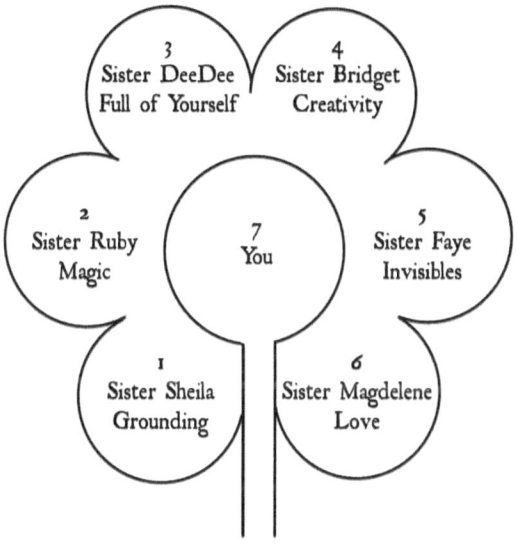

The Mystic Trail Spread

The Old Mermaids General Reading: What's It All About?

This is adapted from a circular reading Vicki Noble discusses in her book *Motherpeace: A Way to the Goddess Through Myth, Art, and Tarot*. Motherpeace is my favorite tarot deck, and it is the one I know best. The Old Mermaids Wisdom Cards is not a tarot deck, but most of the tried and true tarot spreads will work with TOMWC.

Do this reading when you know the cards and what they mean to you, for the most part. You can ask a question or use this as a general reading about what's going on for you now. Remember, TOMWC do not predict the future; they help you navigate your life.

Shuffle the cards any way you like. I shuffle and then cut the deck into three piles and put the third pile on the top. Then I take the cards from the top of that pile.

I would advise you to put all the cards you've chosen face down first and then turn them over one by one. I encourage you to take notes or do whatever will help you remember the reading. Maybe leave the cards out in this shape for a few days.

1. This card answers the question of who you are now.

2. What's happening in your life now: the atmosphere?

3. What is the obstacle or the cross current in your life?

4. How are you feeling physically now? How are you rooted?

5. What is in the recent past that is affecting you now?

6. What is going on in your mind? What are you thinking?

7. What is coming soon if you keep doing what you're doing?

8. What is your self-image?

9. What are your hopes and fears?

10. Who or what is close to you? What is your environment like?

11. What is the resolution or outcome to your question?

12. Now choose two cards randomly. The first card will help you stay grounded and healthy during this time.

13. The second card will help you let go of any obstacles so you can move forward.

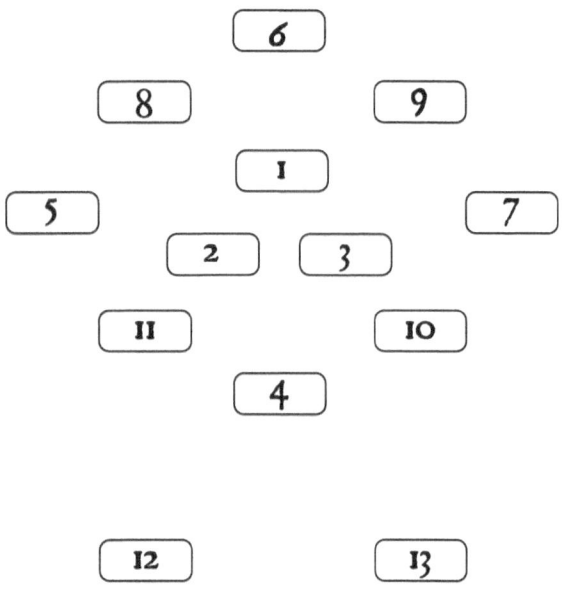

The Old Mermaids General Reading Spread

Index

barometer bush, 46
barrel cactus, 228
black-tailed gnatcatcher, 47
Blueberry Omelet, 154
bobcat, 65
bosques, 200
butterflies, 46
cactus wren, 75, 111
cardinal, 232
cereus cactus, 78
cottonwoods, 178, 224
coyote, 121
datura flower, 49
dawn, 108
deer, 241

desert spoon, 129, 132

Dry Summer
   Grand Mother Yemaya Mermaid, 221
   Mother Star Stupendous Mermaid, 229
   Sister Bea Wilder Mermaid, 59
   Sister Bridget Mermaid, 131
   Sister DeeDee Lightful Mermaid, 47
   Sister Faye Mermaid, 240
   Sister Laughs A Lot Mermaid, 108
   Sister Lyra Musica Mermaid, 78
   Sister Magdelene Mermaid, 193
   Sister Ruby Rosarita Mermaid, 142
   Sister Sheila Na Giggles Mermaid, 38
   Sister Sophia Mermaid, 169
   Sister Ursula Divine Mermaid, 121

Fall
   Grand Mother Yemaya Mermaid, 224
   Mother Star Stupendous Mermaid, 231
   Sister Bea Wilder Mermaid, 67
   Sister Bridget Mermaid, 133
   Sister DeeDee Lightful Mermaid, 49
   Sister Faye Mermaid, 241
   Sister Laughs A Lot Mermaid, 109
   Sister Lyra Musica Mermaid, 83
   Sister Magdelene Mermaid, 200
   Sister Ruby Rosarita Mermaid, 154
   Sister Sheila Na Giggles Mermaid, 40

    Sister Sophia Mermaid, 178
    Sister Ursula Divine Mermaid, 125
front porch, 243
gila monster, 109
Grand Mother Yemaya Mermaid
    Dry Summer, 221
    Fall, 224
    Monsoon, 222
    Spring, 218
    Winter, 224
great horned owl, 167
hat on a hook, 38
hawk, 119
hooded oriole, 60
hummingbird, 137
jackrabbit, 159
javelina, 224
Kuan Yin, 176
labyrinth, 179
lightning, 222
lush desert landscape, 108
mesquite, 200
Monsoon
    Grand Mother Yemaya Mermaid, 222
    Mother Star Stupendous Mermaid, 230
    Sister Bea Wilder Mermaid, 65
    Sister Bridget Mermaid, 132

    Sister DeeDee Lightful Mermaid, 48
    Sister Faye Mermaid, 240
    Sister Laughs A Lot Mermaid, 108
    Sister Lyra Musica Mermaid, 81
    Sister Magdelene Mermaid, 197
    Sister Ruby Rosarita Mermaid, 148
    Sister Sheila Na Giggles Mermaid, 39
    Sister Sophia Mermaid, 176
    Sister Ursula Divine Mermaid, 124
Mother Star Stupendous Mermaid
    Dry Summer, 229
    Fall, 231
    Monsoon, 230
    Spring, 228
    Winter, 232
nest, 133
Night Blooming Cactus, 78
night sky, 231
ocotillos, 169
owl, 167
palm tree, 60, 240
phainopepla, 188
pin cushion cactus, 72
prickly pear cactus, 56
pyrrhuloxia, 232
quail, 218
Queen of the Night Cactus, 78

rabbit, 67
rain, 240
raven, 238
red barrel cactus, 193
red chairs and blue sky, 51
red rocks, 131
saguaro, 221
Sister Bea Wilder Mermaid
    Dry Summer, 59
    Fall, 67
    Monsoon, 65
    Spring, 56
    Winter, 72
Sister Bridget Mermaid
    Dry Summer, 131
    Fall, 133
    Monsoon, 132
    Spring, 129
    Winter, 134
Sister DeeDee Lightful Mermaid
    Dry Summer, 47
    Fall, 49
    Monsoon, 48
    Spring, 46
    Winter, 51
Sister Faye Mermaid
    Dry Summer, 240

    Fall, 241
    Monsoon, 240
    Spring, 238
    Winter, 243
Sister Laughs A Lot Mermaid
    Dry Summer, 108
    Fall, 109
    Monsoon, 108
    Spring, 104
    Winter, 111
Sister Lyra Musica Mermaid
    Dry Summer, 78
    Fall, 83
    Monsoon, 81
    Spring, 75
    Winter, 93
Sister Magdelene Mermaid
    Dry Summer, 193
    Fall, 200
    Monsoon, 197
    Spring, 188
    Winter, 203
Sister Ruby Rosarita Mermaid
    Dry Summer, 142
    Fall, 154
    Monsoon, 148
    Spring, 137

Winter, 159
Sister Sheila Na Giggles Mermaid
   Dry Summer, 38
   Fall, 40
   Monsoon, 39
   Spring, 37
Sister Sophia Mermaid
   Dry Summer, 169
   Fall, 178
   Monsoon, 176
   Spring, 167
   Winter, 179
Sister Ursula Divine Mermaid
   Dry Summer, 121
   Fall, 125
   Monsoon, 124
   Spring, 119
   Winter, 126
snow, 93
spoons, 148
Spring
   Grand Mother Yemaya Mermaid, 218
   Mother Star Stupendous Mermaid, 228
   Sister Bea Wilder Mermaid, 56
   Sister Bridget Mermaid, 129
   Sister DeeDee Lightful Mermaid, 46
   Sister Faye Mermaid, 238

    Sister Laughs A Lot Mermaid, 104
    Sister Lyra Musica Mermaid, 75
    Sister Magdelene Mermaid, 188
    Sister Ruby Rosarita Mermaid, 137
    Sister Sheila Na Giggles Mermaid, 37
    Sister Sophia Mermaid, 167
    Sister Ursula Divine Mermaid, 119
sunflower, 142
Three Ears, 67
tortoise, 132
vermillion flycatcher, 230
vulture, 40
Winter
    Grand Mother Yemaya Mermaid, 224
    Mother Star Stupendous Mermaid, 232
    Sister Bea Wilder Mermaid, 72
    Sister Bridget Mermaid, 134
    Sister DeeDee Lightful Mermaid, 51
    Sister Faye Mermaid, 243
    Sister Laughs A Lot Mermaid, 111
    Sister Lyra Musica Mermaid, 93
    Sister Magdelene Mermaid, 203
    Sister Ruby Rosarita Mermaid, 159
    Sister Sheila Na Giggles Mermaid, 41
    Sister Sophia Mermaid, 179
    Sister Ursula Divine Mermaid, 126

About the Author

Kim Antieau's books include many accounts of the Old Mermaids and their adventures in the Old Sea and the New Desert. Among them are *Church of the Old Mermaids, The Fish Wife,* and *The Blue Tail.* She has also distilled much of the wisdom of the Old Mermaids into several non-fiction books, including *The Old Mermaids Mystery School, The Old Mermaids Book of Days and Nights, The Old Mermaids Oracle.* Her other books include *The Jigsaw Woman, Whackadoodle Times, Ruby's Imagine, Queendom: Feast of the Saints, The Monster's Daughter, Killing Beauty, Coyote Cowgirl, The Salmon Mysteries,* and *Answering the Creative Call.* She lives in the Southwest with her husband, Mario Milosevic.

Kim's writing: kimantieau.com.
Kim's photographs: kimantieau.smugmug.com.

www.ingramcontent.com/pod-product-compliance
Lightning Source LLC
Chambersburg PA
CBHW030147100526
44592CB00009B/166